Charles D. Missar, MLS
Editor

Management of Federally Sponsored Libraries: Case Studies and Analysis

*Pre-publication
REVIEWS,
COMMENTARIES,
EVALUATIONS . . .*

"Each of the federally sponsored libraries profiled in this compilation of case studies provides a practical, in-depth discussion of library operations. The libraries selected for analysis illustrate the diverse nature of federal libraries and the management styles they have developed to respond to agency missions and clienteles. It is an incisive treatment of the challenges facing the federal library manager and the problems associated with administering the library's programs, budgets, and services.

Among the many unique services described are: the national program to provide reading materials for the nation's blind and physically handicapped; the translation of sci-tech information into

More pre-publication
REVIEWS, COMMENTARIES, EVALUATIONS . . .

English by in-house staff at Redstone; the up-to-the-minute tracking of legislation by the Senate Library; and the many exciting projects under development within NLM to develop sophisticated connections to the evolving high-speed research network."

Signe E. Larson
Librarian,
Information Masters;
formerly Chief, Research Services,
U. S. Dept. of the Interior Library,
Washington, DC

"**M**anagement of Federally Sponsored Libraries: Case Studies and Analysis is one of the first books to give us a glimpse at the delivery of library/information services in seven federal departments/agencies ranging from the U.S. Senate to the Federal Reserve to the National Library of Medicine.

The descriptions of the seven libraries were prepared by individuals affiliated with those libraries, and they give us some idea of how those facilities have developed over time. In addition to the libraries already mentioned, the Pentagon Library, the library for the Sixth Circuit of the U.S. Court of Appeals, the Redstone Scientific Information Center, and the National Library Service for the Blind and Physically Handicapped (part of the Library of Congress) are included. The editor, Charles Missar, has over 30 years of experience in a variety of federal library operations. With this background, Missar provides a concluding chapter to put the experiences of these seven libraries into perspective, highlighting managerial issues and concerns faced by all federal libraries. Missar also gives us some idea of how these issues are dealt with differently in federal libraries than in other types of special libraries. This volume is required reading for anyone considering a library career with the federal government. It is also very useful for anyone interested in special libraries, providing an important look at how these seven libraries operate."

William Fisher
Professor,
School of Library
& Information Science,
San Jose State University

More pre-publication
REVIEWS, COMMENTARIES, EVALUATIONS . . .

"This book presents information in some depth about a selection of widely differing libraries in the three branches of the U.S. Government. Students of library management will find a staggering array of organizational styles and cultures. Library managers will read on to compare and contrast with their own experience, and their own managers can find in the editor's summary chapter a useful tutorial. The book, illustrative rather than comprehensive in its selection of examples, raises many questions about what federal libraries have in common. Perhaps not intending to, the authors cause the reader to wonder about how the immense information resources they describe might be used more widely and perhaps more effectively. Taken as a whole, the book can be a powerful stimulus to further increasingly searching exposition and criticism of the federal library and information enterprise."

Joseph C. Donohue
Consultant,
Library and Information Services,
Falls Church, VA

"*Management of Federally Sponsored Libraries* is an undercover guide to the management of library and information resources in the federal sector that punctuates their value to the American public. It presents examples of the integrated complex multi-library systems that are valuable to a wide range of specialized users. Presentations describing the databases of the defense libraries in the Pentagon and Redstone Scientific Technical Information Center are very informative.

The management study is recommended as a must for librarians serving users working in the government arena, whether they be public or general libraries. The coverage of legislative, judicial, and independent government legal collections is pertinent to law libraries. Corporate libraries would find the guide and study of equal value.

More pre-publication
REVIEWS, COMMENTARIES, EVALUATIONS . . .

"The editor is to be congratulated for his forthright and honest discussion of the difficulties placed on federal libraries by the bureaucracy. The libraries encounter obstacles in hiring, retention, and training of personnel. Restraining procedures of accountability of both civil and military origin are a challenge to all federal libraries."

Catherine D. Scott
Retired Chief Reference Librarian,
Smithsonian Institute;
Past President,
Special Libraries Association

"This book brings together in one volume a very interesting selection of federal libraries, some of which are less known than others, allowing readers to glean a great deal of useful information from the way these libraries were set up historically, are managed today, and are planning their future.

What I find most appealing about the case studies is the variety and the type of approach that each library manager demonstrates in his or her field. The case studies cover various types of libraries, such as the United States Senate Library, the Circuit Court Libraries, and the Department of Defense-Army Libraries that serve a very select clientele, making their approach more inward-looking, while libraries such as the ones found at the Redstone Scientific Information Center, the National Library Service for the Blind, the Federal Reserve, and the National Library of Medicine are more outward-looking. The latter appears to have the broadest mandate by reaching out to the individual practitioner located in small rural communities to create a special link offering them the facilities of the largest research library in medicine available today.

Moreover, the informative descriptions of both the internal operations of the libraries covered (pointing in some instances to new and innovative managerial techniques, as well as the leap into the electronic age with the introduction of the electronic super highway) and the changing role of the librarian/information specialist, because of their universal applicability, will be useful to librarians not only in government settings, but also in nongovernment operations."

Anne M. Galler, MS
Associate Professor,
Concordia University,
Montreal, Quebec

More pre-publication
REVIEWS, COMMENTARIES, EVALUATIONS . . .

"**F**or one who believes that the services of federally sponsored libraries are greatly underappreciated and underused and that their internal operations are somewhat of a mystery, this collection of essays about seven federal libraries is a welcome addition to the library and information science professional bookshelf.

The detailed descriptions of the ways these libraries have adapted to new technologies and the specifics as to how they have done it are helpful to those searching for ways to incorporate the constantly changing advances in providing reference services.

From these case studies, valuable management principles can be learned such as the participatory management style that developed from the use of the Association of Research Librarian's Management Review and Analysis Program at the National Library Service for the Blind and Physically Handicapped, as described by its Director, Frank Kurt Cylke. Four major themes have been developed and are in operation: concern for staff, written guidelines and standards, information flow, and planning and implementation.

As an educator, I see a valuable use of this book in exposing students to the vast career opportunities within the federal government. It is the largest single employer of librarians and has much to offer library and information personnel."

Elizabeth W. Stone, PhD
Professor Emerita,
Former Dean, School of Library
and Information Science,
The Catholic University of America,
Washington, DC

The Haworth Press, Inc.

NOTES FOR PROFESSIONAL LIBRARIANS AND LIBRARY USERS

This is an original book title published by The Haworth Press, Inc. Unless otherwise noted in specific chapters with attribution, materials in this book have not been previously published elsewhere in any format or language.

CONSERVATION AND PRESERVATION NOTES

All books published by The Haworth Press, Inc. and its imprints are printed on certified ph neutral, acid free book grade paper. This paper meets the minimum requirements of American National Standard for Information Sciences–Permanence of Paper for Printed Material, ANSI Z39.48-1984.

Management of Federally Sponsored Libraries
Case Studies and Analysis

HAWORTH Special Librarianship Studies
Ellis Mount, Senior Editor

New, Recent, and Forthcoming Titles:

Creative Planning of Special Library Facilities by Ellis Mount

Basics of Law Librarianship by Deborah S. Panella

Management of Federally Sponsored Libraries: Case Studies and Analysis by Charles D. Missar

Management of Federally Sponsored Libraries
Case Studies and Analysis

Charles D. Missar, MLS
Editor

The Haworth Press
New York • London

© 1995 by The Haworth Press, Inc. All rights reserved. No part of this work may be reproduced or utilized in any form or by any means, electronic or mechanical, including photocopying, microfilm and recording, or by any information storage and retrieval system, without permission in writing from the publisher. Printed in the United States of America.

The Haworth Press, Inc., 10 Alice Street, Binghamton, NY 13904-1580

Library of Congress Cataloging-in-Publication Data

Management of federally sponsored libraries : case studies and analysis / Charles D. Missar, editor.
    p.   cm.
   Includes bibliographical references (p.) and index.
   ISBN 1-56024-395-3
    1. Government libraries–United States–Administration. I. Missar, Charles D.
Z675.G7M36 1995
027.5′0973–dc20
                                                                                94-48730
                                                                                   CIP

CONTENTS

About the Editor	ix
Contributors	xi
Foreword *Ellis Mount*	xv
Preface	xvii
Introduction *Charles D. Missar*	1

PART I: LEGISLATIVE BRANCH

Chapter 1. United States Senate Library — 9
Roger K. Haley

Introduction	9
History	10
Location and Size	12
Organization and Staffing	12
The Collection	17
Patrons	20
Services to Users	21
Automation	24
Planning, Funding, and Budgeting	27
Marketing	29

PART II: JUDICIAL BRANCH

Chapter 2. Sixth Circuit Library for the United States Courts — 35
Kathy Joyce Welker

Features Common to All Circuit Libraries	36
National Library Program Implications	36
National Lawbook Ordering Implications	39

National Personnel Policies	40
Space Design and Management	41
National Automation Initiatives	41
Centralized vs. Decentralized Budgeting Implications	42
Sixth Circuit Library System	43
History of Library System	43
Circuit Library Mission	45
Court(s) Served by Library System	45
Library Committees and Library Judges	46
Organizational and Reporting Relationships	46
Managing in a Decentralized Environment	48
Conclusion	49

PART III: EXECUTIVE BRANCH

Chapter 3. Department of Defense: Army Libraries — 57
Louise Nyce

Types of Libraries	57
Policy Direction	58
Cooperative Efforts	58
Army Library Management Office	59
Army Library Institute	59
Electronic Gateway to Army Libraries	60

Chapter 4. The Pentagon Library — 61
Louise Nyce

Historical Development	61
Manager's Responsibilities	61
Library Patrons	62
Access Policy	63
Scope of the Collection	64
Staffing and Organization	65
Pentagon Library Users System	67
CD-ROM Products	67
Fiscal Support	67
Training and Tours	68

Chapter 5. Redstone Scientific Information Center (RSIC)   71
Sybil H. Bullock

Background	71
Planning and Budgeting	72
Services	77
Staff	77
Marketing	79
Evaluation	80

PART IV: INDEPENDENT AGENCIES

Chapter 6. Research Library of the Board of Governors of the Federal Reserve System   85
Ann Roane Clary

Introduction and Description	85
Organization and Staffing	89
Collection Development	92
Planning and Budgeting	93
Management and Training	96
Administrative Support	98
Facilities and Equipment	98
Networking: Two Contexts	100
Marketing and Evaluating	102
Conclusion	104

PART V: NATIONAL LIBRARIES

Chapter 7. National Library Service for the Blind and Physically Handicapped   109
Frank Kurt Cylke

Authority	109
Background	109
Functions and Responsibilities	112
Office of the Director	113
Management	114
Budget	116
Division/Section/Office Functions	117
Materials Development Division	119

Network Division   121
Summary   125

Chapter 8. National Library of Medicine   129
Kent A. Smith
Robert Mehnert

The National Network   129
Computerized Bibliographic Access   136
Management Planning   137
Outreach   139
Research and Development   141

PART VI: CONCLUSIONS

Chapter 9. An Overview of Effective Management in Federal Libraries   149
Charles D. Missar

Bibliography   **157**

Index   **159**

ABOUT THE EDITOR

Charles Donald Missar, MS in LS, AB, is an Information Consultant for Missar Associates in Washington, DC, and an Indexer for CSC Professional Services Group. Mr. Missar has 30 years of experience working in various federal libraries and information centers, including the Library of Congress, the Educational Resources Information Center (ERIC), and the U.S. Department of Education Research Library. He developed and managed the Educational Reference Center, an online ERIC research facility for the U.S. Department of Education, and headed the Educational Research Library for 7 years. He also represented the Library as a member of the Federal Library and Information Center Committee (FLICC) for 8 years. Mr. Missar is a member of the American Library Association, the American Society for Information Science, and the Special Libraries Association.

CONTRIBUTORS

Sybil H. Bullock, MLS, has spent her entire professional career in government technical libraries. She has worked in all functional areas and is currently Director of the Redstone Scientific Information Center, Huntsville, Alabama. She has an MLS from the University of Alabama School of Library and Information Studies and is currently pursuing post-graduate education. She is also a graduate of the Army Management Staff College.

Ann Roane Clary, MLS, graduated from Mary Washington College in 1952 with a BA degree in English and received her Library degree from the Catholic University of America in 1956. She was head librarian at the American National Red Cross, National Headquarters Library from 1955 until 1960, and then moved to the Research Library, Board of Governors of the Federal Reserve System, Washington, DC, where she worked for 31 years, 24 of which she spent as the chief librarian. She retired in January 1992.

Frank Kurt Cylke, MLS, was appointed Director of the National Library Service for the Blind and Physically Handicapped, Library of Congress, on July 9, 1973. He joined the Library in 1970 as Executive Director of the Federal Library Committee, and in April 1972 also assumed the Chairmanship of the U.S. National Libraries Task Force on Cooperative Activities. Mr. Cylke came to the Library from the United States Office of Education where, from 1968 to 1970, he was Chief of the Library and Information Science Research Branch.

Before his federal service, Mr. Cylke was Assistant Librarian of the Providence Public Library. He previously had been head of reference and in charge of public relations at the New Haven, Connecticut Free Public Library, 1962 to 1965, and in the Reference Department, Bridgeport, Connecticut Public Library, 1958 to 1962. He attended the University of Connecticut, where he received a BA degree in 1954. He earned an MLS degree from Pratt Institute, New

York, in 1957, and has undertaken postgraduate work in library administration, systems analysis, and information sciences. Mr. Cylke has received numerous professional and work-related awards.

Roger K. Haley, MLS, is Librarian of the United States Senate Library, where he began his professional career in 1964. He has served as head of the library since 1973.

He is a native of the District of Columbia and resides on Capitol Hill. He completed his undergraduate studies, majoring in English literature, at Georgetown University, and pursued a doctoral program in Russian Studies at its graduate school. He received his Masters in Library Science degree from Maryland University.

Roger has been an active member of the Special Libraries Association since 1976. He has served as Chair of the Social Science Division, as President of the Washington, DC Chapter, and as a member or chair of several Association committees. In June 1993, he was presented with SLA's John Cotton Dana Award for contributions to special librarianship.

Robert Mehnert, BA, has been the Public Information Officer of the National Library of Medicine since 1971. His earlier positions within the Department of Health and Human Services have been with the Public Health Service, National Institutes of Health, and the National Institute of Mental Health. He is a 1963 graduate of the University of Buffalo with a BA in English Literature.

Louise Nyce, BS, MLS, began her career as an Army Librarian in France and Germany and then moved to Thailand as Command Librarian, where she built libraries and a library program. Five years later she became Command Librarian in Japan, followed by a lengthy tour as Library Program Director for U.S. Army Forces Command, located in Atlanta, Georgia. She became Director of the U.S. Army War College Library in 1986, coming to Washington, DC to be Library Program Director for Army Material Command two years later. She became Pentagon Library Director in 1991.

Kent A. Smith, BA, MA, is the Deputy Director of the National Library of Medicine. As such, he assists the Director in planning and managing the biomedical communications programs of the

NLM. He graduated from Hobart College in 1960 and the Johnson School of Management at Cornell University in 1962.

Kathy Joyce Welker, MLS, has been the Circuit Librarian for the U.S. Court of Appeals for the Sixth Circuit since 1984. From 1976 to 1984 she was the Assistant Director of the Indiana University Law School Library in Indianapolis. Ms. Welker was admitted to the Ohio Bar in 1985. Both her law degree and masters degree in library science are from Indiana University.

Foreword

The concept of preparing a collection of papers on the management of federal libraries was one that Charles Missar, the editor of this book, readily accepted when we first discussed the possibility of his serving as editor of such a work. His success in obtaining papers from a group of distinguished librarians should make this book useful to librarians and information professionals in a wide sphere of disciplines, for those readers with wide experience in their profession as well as for students just starting to get acquainted with the broad spectrum of libraries and information centers in existence.

The breadth of the chapters ranges from the U.S. Congress to the Federal Reserve System, and from major health science organizations to important military establishments, as well as the powerful Federal courts. Together the seven libraries covered in this book touch on the lives of all of us in one way or the other.

The tone of the chapters was purposely chosen to present down-to-earth discussions of what actually happens in the course of business in these libraries. Although principles of management are discussed, the fact that the chapters show how the managers of these libraries apply these basic principles to the operation of these major libraries will be more beneficial to readers than would a mere repetition of basic managerial areas of concern. The scope of the services they offer and the breadth of the clienteles benefitting from these libraries is truly outstanding. Together they have holdings of over five million titles of books and reports, tens of thousands of different media, and countless types of computer-based products. Further, electronic networks link them to other libraries and institutions.

This book includes a chapter by Charles Missar in which he summarizes the responsibilities of federal librarians and provides an insightful overview of ways to meet the goals and requirements in such organizations. His years of experience are evident in this chapter.

Thus, this book serves a worthy purpose in providing a record of the variety of information services being offered by several types of federal libraries in this country. It occupies a unique position as being possibly the first compilation to deal in depth with libraries of this sort.

Ellis Mount, DLS
Editor, Haworth Special Librarianship Studies

Preface

In checking recent library science literature, it was immediately evident that there is a dearth of publications dealing with the management of federal libraries. Because of my experience over three decades in a variety of federal libraries, I was encouraged to invite several federal library managers to write a chapter about their facilities which would be helpful, instructional, and informative. In addition to serving as editor of this volume, I prepared a summary chapter which analyzes the various papers.

I want to thank each of the contributing authors for cooperating so willingly in this effort despite already heavy demands on their time. Also, it is a pleasure to acknowledge Dr. Ellis Mount's encouragement and direction from the very beginning of the project, and especially to recognize my son, David, for his preparation of several diskettes and my wife, Margaret Mary, for her technical support and editorial expertise.

Introduction

Charles D. Missar

The concept of management conjures up many activities relating to the operation of a business or a service. These include planning and budgeting, organizing and directing, staffing, supervising, and evaluating. All of these are action words, which imply doing something related to an overall objective. For the purpose of this monograph, it is the matter of running a library effectively and efficiently. Since a library is a complex business/service made up of many activities, it is necessary to understand something about the various parts and how they interact with each other.

Customarily, libraries are organized into two major divisions: public services and technical services. The public services portion usually includes reference and referrals, circulation, and interlibrary loan. In today's environment it also often encompasses search negotiations, online searching, and information packaging. Information services broaden this to include not only books and periodicals, but also technical reports and statistical information as well as newspaper articles, and even audio and video tapes.

The technical services staff is basically concerned with behind-the-scenes activities. These include the acquisition of all types of library materials, cataloging and classifying each of the items, and then making certain that the identifying information is available and usable in card or printed catalogs, on microform readers, in online databases, or on compact disks. Technicians are also responsible for arranging these materials in appropriate files, cabinets, or on shelves so that they can be conveniently browsed or quickly retrieved. While selection of materials is frequently shared by all professional staff, most present-day libraries have a collections development specialist who has overall responsibility for this task. In addition, most libraries have a systems specialist to provide technical help with all matters related to computer applications. The importance of this position must not be underestimated since most libraries are now using online services, bibliographic utilities, CD-ROM diskette equipment, and microform readers and printers.

From the point of view of the head of the library these are all areas of responsibility and concern. The purpose of this book is to provide an insight into how several federal managers view their roles and carry out their duties.

Federal library management is influenced by many factors. Obviously the organizational position of the library has a major impact on how it is managed. In some cases, support for the library is a high priority, and it is positioned in the bureaucratic structure so that it can receive financial support as well as visibility. In other cases, the library is buried in the organizational chart where it can be ignored or can even operate with virtual independence. Even in this less-than-desirable situation, however, the financial support can often be reasonable, and the program developed by the imagination of the manager.

Federal libraries have operated and still continue to function across this broad spectrum today–from highly visible to almost hidden in the agency. However, with the recent emphasis on information services, the library is in a position to take on a more forceful role. In many agencies a close look is currently being taken at the library's function and operations. Moreover, the use of technologies, such as online searching services, computerized catalogs, compact disk storage and retrieval, and personal computers has caught the attention of higher level management both because of exciting new applications for the technology itself, and because of the increased cost associated with the resulting products and services.

Federally sponsored libraries are a large and diverse group. According to the *Directory of Federal Libraries* (Oryx Press, 1993, 2nd edition), there are 2,516 such facilities, most of which are traditional libraries or parts of libraries providing a variety of information services. They are arranged under branches of the Federal Government, with the number of entries as follows:

Legislative Branch	–	43
Judicial Branch	–	96
Executive Branch	–	2,052
Independent Agencies	–	325

In further reviewing this list, it was found that the Departments of Defense and the Interior had the largest numbers, 967 and 604 entries, respectively. Other Executive Branch departments with significant numbers of libraries include:

Veterans Affairs	–	165
Justice	–	87
Commerce	–	71
Agriculture	–	54
Energy	–	30
Health & Human Services	–	26

Since there are such large numbers under the Departments of Defense and Interior it is helpful to break out the various subgroups.
For Defense, the breakout by branch is:

Army	–	462
Navy	–	257
Air Force	–	190
Marine Corps	–	25
Joint Services	–	33

Of this total, 192 are located overseas.
For Interior, the larger listings are:

National Park Service	–	303
Bureau of Indian Affairs	–	186

Bureau of Land
  Management — 48
Geological Survey — 21

Under Independent Agencies, those with large numbers are:

U.S. Information Agency — 155
Environmental Protection
  Agency — 28
Smithsonian Institution — 24
Federal Reserve System — 17
National Aeronautics and
  Space Administration — 14
National Archives and
  Records Administration — 13

The federal government also supports a number of Presidential Libraries through the National Archives and Records Administration. Starting with President Herbert Hoover (1929-1933), there are eleven such libraries:

Herbert Hoover Presidential Library, West Branch, IA
Franklin D. Roosevelt Library, Hyde Park, NY
Harry S. Truman Library, Independence, MO
Dwight D. Eisenhower Library, Abilene, KS
John F. Kennedy Library, Boston, MA
Lyndon B. Johnson Library, Austin, TX
Richard M. Nixon Library, Yorba Linda, CA
Gerald R. Ford Library, Ann Arbor, MI
Jimmy Carter Library, Atlanta, GA
Ronald Reagan Presidential Library, Simi Valley, CA
George H. W. Bush Library, College Station, TX

These are basically major research facilities with large collections of materials relevant to the term of each president and staffed with trained professionals.

The federal government also supports three officially recognized national libraries: the Library of Congress, National Agricultural Library, and the National Library of Medicine. The National Library Services for the Blind and Physically Handicapped is also a national program, but organizationally it is attached to the Library of Congress. Each of the institutions is adequately provided with funds and staff to carry out its various national responsibilities.

Through the Bureau of Indian Affairs (U.S. Department of the Interior) and the Overseas Dependent Schools (U.S. Department of Defense), the federal government provides support for elementary and secondary school libraries. It also provides library services at the military academies and at other higher educational facilities supported by the Department of Defense and the Bureau of Indian Affairs. There are also libraries at training centers supported by the Departments of State, Treasury, and Defense, and by the Federal Bureau of Investigation (U.S. Department of Justice).

Both the Departments of Veterans Affairs and of Defense support libraries for patients in their hospitals, while libraries for those confined to penal institutions are supported through the Bureau of Prisons (U.S. Department of Justice). A significant number of federal libraries focus on science, engineering, health, and medicine, accounting for approximately 20 percent of the total. But almost one-half of the 2,516 facilities listed in the *Directory* are classified as either general or special types and are not included in any of the above-described categories.

This broad array of federally sponsored libraries reflects the areas of interest, concern, or responsibility of various federal agencies. The need for library and information services is indicated or implied though the above-mentioned *Directory*. The degree of support and the type of management is the focus of this book.

In studying the data presented in the *Directory*, it is clear that many libraries are minimally supported with staff and resources. A fairly large number have only one professional librarian, who often serves with or without clerical or technical help. Many of these one-person libraries provide a very special service to a very limited number of people, either because they are in remote locations, are used by a small number of patrons, or are satellites of a larger library.

From the vast list of federally supported libraries it was decided to select just seven to serve as case studies–not to reflect all the different types of facilities but to give a cross section of various types. From the national perspective, the National Library of Medicine (NLM), and the National Library Service for the Blind and Physically Handicapped (NLS/BPH) were selected. The first organization is part of the U.S. Department of Health and Human Services and a major component of the National Institutes of Health, while the NLS/BPH is under the Assistant Librarian for National Programs at the Library of Congress (LC). Kent Smith, Deputy Director at NLM, addresses management issues for his facility, and F. Kurt Cylke, Director of NLS/BPH, does the same for the LC component.

The Research Library of the Federal Reserve System (FRS) was selected as an example of a facility serving a quasi-independent agency. It is a stand-alone library established to serve the needs of the members of the FRS in Washington, DC. Ann Clary, the former director, discusses her role as manager, covering a period of some 20 years, during which many changes were occurring in the federal library community.

From the Judicial Branch, Kathy Welker, librarian for the Sixth Circuit of the U.S. Court of Appeals, was selected. Headquartered in Cincinnati, this library, with its satellite branches, is fairly typical of the libraries in the other eleven circuits.

Representing the Legislative Branch of the government is the U.S. Senate Library. Roger Haley discusses his role as manager of this very specialized facility.

Finally, the Executive Branch is represented by two Department of Defense libraries. Louise Nyce, the librarian at the Pentagon Library, Arlington, VA, and Sybil Bullock, Director of the Redstone Scientific Information Center, Huntsville, AL, cooperated on the chapter discussing U.S. Army libraries in general, and discussed their two facilities in particular.

PART I:
LEGISLATIVE BRANCH

Chapter 1

United States Senate Library

Roger K. Haley

INTRODUCTION

The library of the United States Senate is a legislative and general reference library which provides both traditional and computerized information services and which maintains a comprehensive collection of congressional, governmental, monographic, serial, and other publications. The general mission of the library is to provide information and the use of its resources to members of the Senate and to Senate staff, Senate and House committees, and other authorized users.

The library's principal functions are designed to carry out this general mission and include the following:

- to offer traditional library services–legislative research, general reference and quick reference, book loans, binding, reader assistance and a reading room for Senators, Senate staff, and other authorized users;
- to provide up-to-date information on the status of pending legislation through an in-house database known as Senate LEGIS;
- to maintain a collection of congressional and government publications, and materials relating to the specialized interests of the library: government and politics, history, biography, economics, international relations, and general reference works;
- to maintain a catalog and shelflist of its collections, and to provide library materials to Senate offices.

HISTORY

As early as the Second United States Congress meeting in Philadelphia in 1791-1792, the Senate adopted a resolution directing the Secretary of the Senate "to procure, and deposit in his office, the laws of the several states" for the use of Senators. This action is regarded as the foundation of today's library. In the decades between 1820 and 1850, the Chief Clerk of the Senate, William Hickey, working under the Secretary of the Senate, began collecting copies of printed bills and resolutions, committee reports of legislation, and other Senate documents. As this collection of materials grew, Hickey urged the establishment of a library in order to manage and maintain the materials. There were several unsuccessful efforts to create the library during these years, and it was not until 1870-1871 that it was formally established as a department under the jurisdiction of the Secretary of the Senate. The Senate adopted a resolution designating a suite of rooms in the Capitol for use as a library, and in 1871 the first Senate Librarian, George S. Wagner, was appointed. Wagner took over the collection of legislative documents accumulated by Hickey, organized it, cataloged it, and continued to maintain it, as did Wagner's successors.

By the end of the nineteenth century, the collection had grown considerably, and the rooms set aside for the library were no longer able to hold all the materials. Early in the 1900s, an attic area of the Capitol above the library's space was constructed and fitted for the library's use with installation of steel shelving. The addition of this space not only permitted the continued accumulation of legislative and other legal materials, but also allowed for the acquisition of different kinds of materials not previously collected. By the 1950s, the library had developed an extensive book collection as well as publications of the executive branch of the government, and periodical and newspaper titles.

In the late 1960s and early 1970s the library began a microform collection and started to acquire access to automated databases, among them retrieval systems for news and journal items, government documents, legal research, and bibliographic citations. In the 1990s, newer technologies were also adopted, including CD-ROM and optical disks.

Photo 1.1. U.S. Capitol, West Front. The Senate Library is located in the left wing, third floor, distinguished by the center circular window. Courtesy of the Architect of the Capitol.

LOCATION AND SIZE

The Senate Library is situated in the oldest portion of the Senate wing of the Capitol (see Photo 1.1). It is on the west side of the building with a view overlooking the Mall, and it occupies the same three rooms on the third floor that were originally assigned over 120 years ago when the library was established. These rooms consist of the Senators' Reading Room, the reference room, and the librarian's office. In addition, there is an extensive area on the fourth floor to accommodate book storage and support staff.

These spaces provide a total of approximately 9,000 square feet; shelving in the library totals about 11,000 linear feet. This capacity, however, is insufficient to house the entire collection. As a result, the library maintains two off-site storage areas to house certain older materials that are less frequently used, as well as duplicate materials that serve as a reserve for certain portions of the collection.

In 1989 a decision was made to relocate the library to the nearby Senate office buildings to provide more adequate space, to reunify the collection, and to place the facility more conveniently for the majority of its users. Planning and design work began in 1992, and the new library is expected to open in 1996. Two of the original rooms in the Capitol will be retained as a branch office to serve the Senate chamber and leadership offices.

ORGANIZATION AND STAFFING

The Senate Library is one of a score of departments and offices under the jurisdiction of the Secretary of the Senate, who is elected by the Senate and serves as its chief administrator and financial officer. The departments under the Secretary's direction include floor clerks such as the Parliamentarian, the Legislative Clerk, the Journal Clerk, and others, through whose hands pass the documents produced in the course of the legislative process; a number of service organizations such as the Document Room, the Senate Library, the Historical Office, the Public Records Office, and others; and the Disbursing Office, which is responsible for the financial activities of the Senate.

U.S. SENATE LIBRARY
ORGANIZATION CHART
October 1993

ADMINISTRATION
Librarian   Secretary
Assistant Librarian

SUPPORT SERVICES

| Library Automation Coordinator | Legis Validation Clerk |

TECHNICAL SERVICES

Head Cataloger   Cong. Documents Clk.
Cataloger/Acq. Librn. Govt. Documents Clk.
Cataloger   Library Aide
Cat./Acq. Technician   Library Aide
Cataloging Technician Library Aide

INFORMATION SERVICES

References	**Legis**
Head Ref. Librn.	Head Legis Ref. Asst.
Ref. Librn.	Legis. Ref. Asst.
Ref. Librn.	Legis. Ref. Asst.
Ref. Asst.	Legis. Ref. Asst.

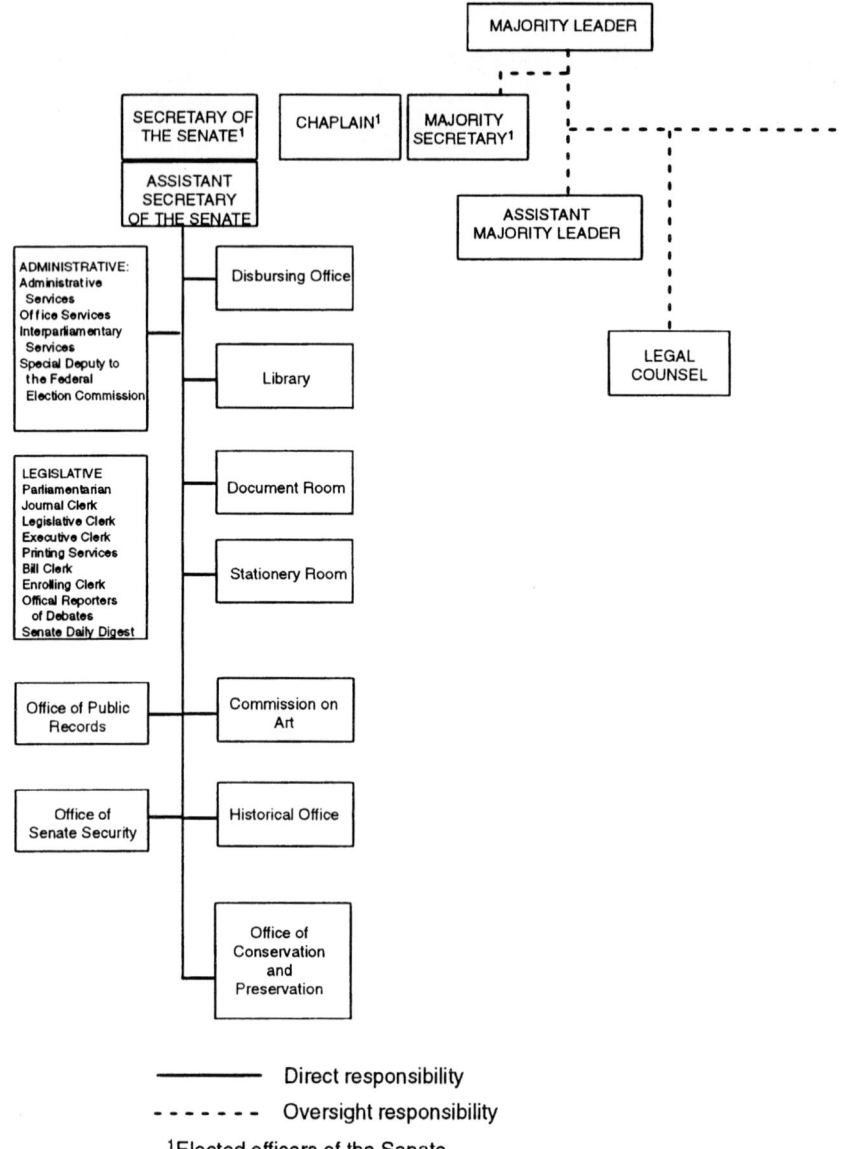

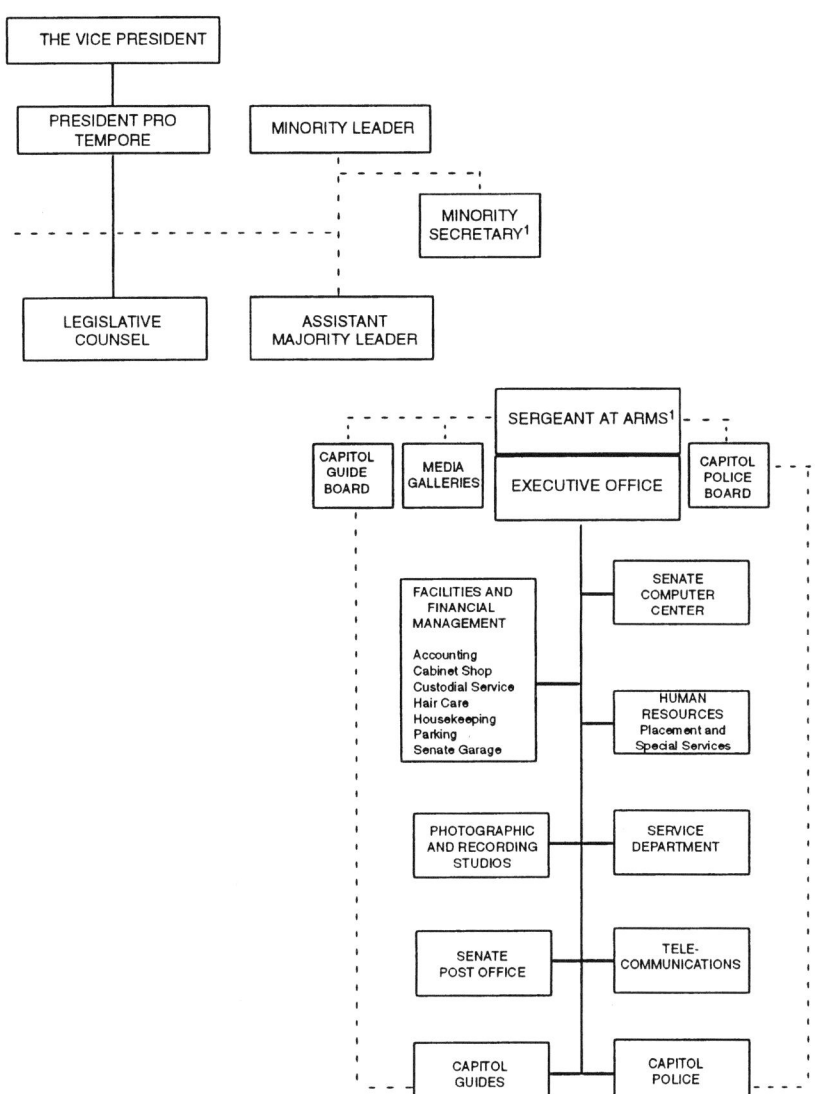

The library staff totals 23 people who are organized along functional lines into four separate areas: administration, information services, technical services, and technical support. There are ten professional librarians on the staff, assigned across all four functional areas. The administration of the library's operations is conducted by the Senate Librarian and the assistant librarian. The information services consist of two groups: the reference section and the LEGIS section. Five librarians work in the reference section under the direction of the head reference librarian; four legislative reference assistants work in the LEGIS section under the direction of the head legislative reference assistant.

Technical services is comprised of ten people, including catalogers, an acquisitions librarian, cataloging technicians, and library aides, all supervised by the head cataloger. Technical support is provided by a library automation coordinator and a LEGIS validation clerk. Finally, there is a secretary for the library who serves the librarian and the rest of the staff. Day-to-day supervision of the staff is provided by the respective section heads, each of whom reports to the assistant librarian and to the librarian, as do the two technical support positions. The librarian and assistant librarian provide overall direction and coordination.

A major change in the composition of the staff occurred in the 1970s. Prior to that time, selection of staff was made extensively on a patronage basis. Vacancies were filled by individual Senators who controlled certain positions in the library which were assigned to them on the basis of their seniority. Consequently, appointments to most library positions were made with minimal consideration of qualifications. In the mid-1970s, this practice gradually changed as the need for professionalism became recognized coincident with the growing use of automation in library operations. This emphasis on hiring qualified professionals has resulted in the development of a very able and highly skilled staff dedicated to service.

The policy of the Office of the Secretary dictates that performance evaluations be done every other year. In the library these evaluation reviews are conducted by the librarian and assistant librarian together with the appropriate section head. The reviews are regarded as an opportunity to assess a staff member's contribution to the total operation and to measure his or her effectiveness.

Evaluations consist of an interview between the supervisors and the employee, and result in a written evaluation of the employee's work performance. A copy of the evaluation is provided to the employee as well as included in the personnel files in the Secretary's Office. These assessments are considered primarily a management tool to improve performance and productivity, and also serve as a factor in determining salary levels. In practice, however, the formal evaluation process only supplements the ongoing supervision provided to employees on a day-to-day basis. If a performance problem develops, it is quickly noted, and every effort is made to remedy the situation as soon as possible.

There is now a heavy emphasis on professional recruitment and development. The hiring process for both professional and nonprofessional positions places a strong value on qualifications and experience, and has produced the development of a highly skilled staff dedicated to service. Once appointed, appropriate staff training is provided to maintain and enhance these skills, both on the job and by means of in-house and external seminars and workshops. The library's budget provides funding for participation in programs of training and continuing education. In addition, membership in professional library associations is encouraged; administrative leave is permitted to provide time to engage in the activities of local professional groups, and travel funds made available for attendance at library association conferences. Staff members are also encouraged to pursue appropriate degree programs at local universities.

THE COLLECTION

The Senate Library's active collection totals about 100,000 volumes with another 50,000 in off-site storage.

Collection Development Policy. Collection development is guided by a written policy to foster the acquisition of materials relating to the particular interests of the Senate Library. The policy therefore emphasizes the importance of such topics as political biography, American history, political science, government and politics, as well as economics and international relations. The receipt of all printed legislative records is a requirement of the policy, and this program is furthered by the fact that many of the materials received by the library are obtained as a matter of law. In addition to congressional publications, the library acquires many government publications issued by executive branch departments, agencies, boards, commissions, and bureaus. Collection of these materials is achieved primarily through participation in the Superintendent of Documents' government depository library program. As a selective library, collection development focuses on the annual reports of executive branch departments, decisions of regulatory agencies, other serial publications, reports of special commissions, and statistical data.

The reference collection policy calls for acquisition of encyclopedias, almanacs and yearbooks, works on statistical materials, and historical, biographical, geographical, political, legal, and bibliographic resources; it also promotes an extensive collection of quotation anthologies.

The practical application of the collection development policy begins with review, by the acquisitions librarian, of various publishers' catalogs, book review publications and library journals, and brochures and notices from publishers. The acquisitions librarian culls likely candidates for purchases from these evaluations, and final selections are made by the reference librarians. The acquisitions librarian then places orders with local book dealers and with national jobbers.

Legislative Records. The core of the library's holdings is a nearly complete collection of the printed documents of the Senate and the House of Representatives which have been produced in the course of the legislative process. This collection runs from the earliest Congresses to the present time, and includes bills and resolutions, hearings of congressional committees and committee prints, the *U.S. Congressional Serial Set* (which comprises the numbered reports accompanying legislation and the numbered documents of the House and Senate), as well as the record of floor proceedings as contained in the official journals of each chamber and in the records of debate as published in the Congressional Record and its predecessors. The culmination of this process is, of course, the law, which is published in the *United States Statutes at Large* and in the codified version of the law, the *United States Code*.

Legal Works. The library is primarily a legislative library, although its holdings include legal materials, such as the *United*

States Code Annotated, United States Reports, the *Federal Supplement,* and numerous treatises, encyclopedias, and law review journals. It does not maintain the national reporter system of cases.

Government Publications. Another important portion of the library's collection is that of government publications, which consists of an extensive collection of about 7,500 titles of publications from the executive branch, largely serial in nature. It includes the *Federal Register* and *Code of Federal Regulations,* White House press releases, the annual reports of most of the executive departments, and decisions of regulatory agencies and executive courts. The library was designated as a government depository library in 1979 to foster systematic selection of those types of government publications best suited to the needs of its users in the Senate.

Books and Periodicals. The book collection contains over 14,000 titles and consists primarily of political biographies and published papers of Senators, Presidents, and other key political figures, as well as works on history, political science, international relations, economics, and general reference works. The library also receives about a dozen major daily and weekly newspapers and subscribes to over 200 periodicals, magazines, and journals.

Non-Print Materials. Among its non-print resources, the library holds an extensive microform collection of congressional documents, and magazines and newspapers; it now totals over one million microfiche and over 6,000 reels of microfilm. Users may read the materials on equipment in the library's micrographics center and/or may obtain hard copy printouts or duplicate fiche.

Other non-print media augmenting the library's resources include optical disk and CD-ROM technologies. The library participates in the Library of Congress' optical disk system, which stores large amounts of text of public policy journal articles. This text can be produced on demand in its original print format. CD-ROM also offers compact storage of large quantities of statistical, bibliographic, and textual data which can be searched and manipulated by means of personal computers. More recently, the library has begun an audiovisual collection consisting primarily of videos on topics relating to the legislative process, the Capitol, and government operations.

Collection Preservation. With the cooperation of the Office of Conservation and Preservation, another department under the Secretary of the Senate, library management developed in 1981 a written plan to guide actions taken in response to a water or fire disaster. It is entitled *U.S. Senate Library Disaster Preparedness and Recovery Plan* and has been revised and updated four times since its original drafting. There has been one occasion when these guidelines have proved their value–in 1988 a roof leak in an off-site storage area resulted in a soaking of several hundred volumes; a swift and vigorous effort, using response options outlined in the plan, salvaged most of them for future use.

In more recent years, the library has become more conscious of the need for long-term planning for collection preservation. In 1993 a consultant in conservation inspected the library's collections and prepared a detailed report analyzing their condition and recommending options for action which will be very useful in drafting a formal policy and systematic preservation program.

PATRONS

As a special library, the Senate Library is reserved primarily for the use of the Senate. More specifically, the library serves present and former Senators, and permanent staff members in Senators' offices and in Senate committees. In addition, the library serves the officers and staff of the Secretary of the Senate and of the Sergeant at Arms of the Senate, as well as the leadership offices of the Senate. This primary user group totals about 7,000 people.

The library cooperates on a reciprocal basis, and to the extent possible, with all offices of the Congress and with the other branches of the federal government as well as with the library community in general. It does not, however, participate in interlibrary loan programs on a formal basis. Among these secondary constituencies are included the members and the leadership offices of the House of Representatives, permanent staff of the House, the House Library, and the Architect of the Capitol.

With regard to the executive branch, the Senate Library cooperates with the Library of the Executive Office of the President and with the offices of the various departments and agencies of the federal government. In the judicial branch, the library works closely with the Library of the Supreme Court.

The Senate Library may be used on a limited basis by journalists accredited to the Senate press galleries. It is generally closed to the public unless specific authorization is obtained in writing; a letter signed by a Senator is required and will be honored for legitimate research in materials available only in the library's collection.

The Senate Library is often confused with the Library of Congress, yet they are distinct libraries. While both operate as units within the legislative branch, the Senate Library is specifically part of the Senate while the Library of Congress serves not only the federal legislature but also a broader national and international constituency. The division within the Library of Congress that most closely operates along the lines of the Senate Library is the Congressional Research Service (CRS), a very large information resource whose services are available only to the Congress.

Although some of the capabilities and services of CRS and of the Senate Library overlap, a main distinction between them is that CRS is both a reference and a research organization, while the Senate Library is essentially a reference service. Because the scope of its subject area is concentrated and specialized, the Senate Library typically can provide information and documentation more quickly than CRS; on the other hand, the Senate Library is unable to provide the in-depth research and analysis that CRS routinely handles. As a practical matter, the two information services operate in close collaboration and commonly direct inquiries from one to the other depending on the nature of the inquiry.

SERVICES TO USERS

The library's hours of operation are 9:00 a.m. to 5:30 p.m. Monday through Friday. In addition to these normal hours, the library is also open and staffed whenever the Senate is in session. Late evening hours occur frequently, and weekend service is occasionally required, usually during the closing weeks of a session.

The Senate Library offers a wide range of services, all of which are available to its primary users and, on a more limited basis, to its secondary users as well. It is the policy of the Secretary of the Senate that library services are provided on a non-partisan basis; the library staff strives to maintain a consistent, professional, and unbiased level of service regardless of party affiliation. Costs of services are not charged back to users, but rather are borne by the Office of the Secretary through the library's budget.

The most important function of the library is to provide information services, which are divided into two sections–the reference service and the LEGIS service. The former is staffed by experienced reference librarians who perform legislative, and to a lesser extent, legal reference, as well as general reference. In 1992 this section processed over 18,500 inquiries, significantly above the 16,000 annual average of the preceding five years. Typically, these requests are for legislative materials, provisions of law and government regulations, biographical information, background information on a wide variety of topics, computer searches of newspaper and magazine articles, quotations, and voting information and statistics. The subject matter reflects the major events and public policy issues that confront the Congress each year. In 1992, for example, topics of domestic interest included campaign reform, constitutional amendments on congressional pay and on a balanced federal budget, voter registration, abortion, health care, family and medical leave, enterprise zones, unemployment and civil rights. Topics of foreign interest embraced most-favored-nation status for China, events in the Middle East, Somalia, and the former Yugoslavia, and aid to Russia and the former soviet republics.

The LEGIS section is staffed by highly trained nonprofessionals who use the Senate LEGIS system, an in-house database which tracks the status of legislation pending before the Congress. Most inquiries are for information about the subject matter, sponsorship, and legislative status of bills, resolutions, and public laws; about Senate action on treaties and nominations; and about scheduling of Senate committee hearings. The LEGIS service is the library's most popular specialty, with over 73,500 calls in 1992; the average number of calls per year during the five prior years was almost 71,500. Inquiries are answered while the caller is on the phone with one of the legislative reference assistants and usually take only a few minutes to conclude. Reference inquiries, on the other hand, take more time to answer and typically require materials to be retrieved from the collection; nevertheless, the reference librarians attempt to provide same-day or next-day service.

Materials needed by users are readily provided either by photocopying from the library's collections, by printouts from automated databases, or by loans of items. Virtually everything in the library is permitted to circulate, although reference materials are lent out only overnight.

Patrons who wish to come to the library may use the Senators' Reading Room, a pleasant room adjacent to the reference section where users can work in a secluded area away from distractions and interruptions. There were more than 7,000 visitors to the Reading Room in 1992. Since the bookstacks on the floor above are closed, readers requiring materials from the shelves are supplied with them by library aides. When circumstances warrant, however, arrangements can be made for users to browse the bookstacks if the particular nature of the search is best suited by that alternative.

The technical services staff also provide a vital contribution to the community of users by performing the less visible tasks relating to acquisitions, technical processing, and cataloging. In 1983 the library converted its card catalog to an in-house online system which employed the software of the Library of Congress' Computerized Catalog. This modified version was dubbed the Senate Library Computerized Catalog (SLCC), and has proven to be very successful.

Since its inception, SLCC has been on the mainframe computer of the Senate Computer Center and is thus available in all Senate offices as one of the files in the Senate LEGIS system. SLCC currently contains approximately 55,000 bibliographic records and includes all current acquisitions of monographs, government documents, and congressional committee hearings and committee prints. A retrospective cataloging of the monograph collection and the government documents collection gradually has been completed, and a retrospective cataloging of the committee print collection has been underway since 1985. The task of retrospectively cataloging committee hearings remains a future project. In 1992 the technical services staff produced more than 7,000 bibliographic records of both currently acquired items and retrospective items.

Another service offered to patrons is the library's micrographics center, which is located on the fourth floor in a room used solely for the storage and use of microforms. Here are housed three microfiche/microfilm reader/printers, as well as storage cabinets for approximately one million fiche and over 6,000 reels of microfilm accumulated by the library in the last 25 years. The materials collected in microform are primarily of two sorts. First, virtually all of the legislative records of the Congress which the library collects in paper are also kept in microform. This practice serves two purposes: the microform backup can be used if a particular volume is not on the shelf; and, the library is able to store some of the older and less used portions of the printed legislative records in off-site storage. The second group of microforms consists primarily of selected newspapers and popular magazines. This compact form of storage permits the library to keep many more years of these materials than would otherwise be possible in paper.

The micrographics center is used primarily to reproduce pages of text from the film micro-image by means of the reader/printers; in 1992 almost 3,500 pages were printed. Another capability of the service provides duplication of microfiche from the library's masters; the library will loan portable readers to patrons who wish to take advantage of this option.

AUTOMATION

As stated above, one of the most influential changes in the library in the last 20 years has been the professionalization of the staff; a second has been the introduction of automation, which has produced significant improvements in the quality of service offered, and in productivity. In the mid-1970s the library's first step in the direction of automation was the effort to provide legislative tracking for Senate offices. Indeed, the first legislative tracking system utilized in the Senate Library was a database developed by the House of Representatives. Two years after its introduction, it was replaced by the Senate LEGIS system which has been refined and expanded in the years since, and now offers up-to-date information on the status of legislation pending before both Houses as well as many other files: information on nominations, treaties, votes, the Senate Library's online catalog, and others. This system is maintained by the Senate Computer Center and is available to all Senate offices.

The library also has access to databases maintained by the House Information Services (HIS). These databases include the House LEGIS system, the full text of bills and resolutions, House votes, the *United States Code*, and news databases such as AP Newswire and Reuter.

Thirdly, the library has access to SCORPIO (Subject-Content-Oriented Retriever for Processing Information Online), the principal database of the Library of Congress, which includes such files as the Library of Congress Computerized Catalog and other bibliographic files, online Issue Briefs, CRS Reports, and public policy literature.

Beginning in 1976, the library began to acquire access to a number of commercial databases which are paid for by the library's computer services budget. The vendors of these systems have varied through the years beginning with the New York Times Information Bank. The most used of these subscription services are various news files, as well as Dialog and legal databases. At the present time, the library subscribes to Burrelle's, DataTimes, Dialog, LegiSlate, Mead Data Central (for Nexis and Lexis), Westlaw, and Wilsonline. The reference librarians used these systems to make over 5,200 searches in 1992.

To maintain its online catalog, the library uses the bibliographic services of the Online Computer Library Center (OCLC) to which the library subscribes through FEDLINK. The latter was established in 1976 under the auspices of the Federal Library and Information Center Committee (FLICC) within the Library of Congress to provide centralized services to the federal library and information center community as well as to other federal activities. Its services include access to online database retrieval systems, bibliographic utilities, and the services of book wholesalers and serials subscription agents.

The Senate Library's technical services staff search the OCLC database for the catalog records of most newly acquired titles, edit and produce these records, and receive the data on a weekly tape from OCLC; original cataloging is performed when OCLC records are not available. The weekly tape is mounted on the Senate Computer Center's mainframe, and its records are merged with the Senate Library Computerized Catalog file.

In May 1990 the library developed an in-house automated system for its circulation records to replace its manual system. It is designed on Paradox software and, while not integrated with the online catalog, it has been a distinct success.

After several years of investigation and planning, the library acquired in 1993 an integrated library system which is expected to provide a marked improvement over the in-house systems in use for the last ten years. The system chosen was DataTrek, and its procurement was a significant milestone in the library's long-range automation plan; conversion to the new system represents a major challenge for the staff. DataTrek offers modules for cataloging, circulation, acquisitions, serials control, and an online public access catalog. The MARC (Machine Readable Cataloging) records in SLCC will be imported into the DataTrek catalog module, and item records for every volume will also be created for the circulation module to permit barcoding of the collection.

Other automated technologies employed by the library include CD-ROM and optical disk. The library's first CD-ROM products were obtained in 1992, and more are expected to be acquired each year as the CD-ROM line item in the budget can be increased. The types of products obtained are usually reference materials and suitable publications available through the government depository program.

The library's use of optical disk technology relies on the system developed and installed in 1990 by the Library of Congress. This system permits CRS and congressional staff to view and print documents included in the CRS Public Policy Literature Database and the CRS Products File. Optical disk workstations, consisting of personal computers and printers linked in a network by highspeed optical fiber, are located in various reader services facilities both in the Library of Congress buildings and in the House and Senate office buildings, including the Senate Library in the Capitol. Over 60,000 documents, stored in the database by means of optical scanners, are in the system and are searchable and retrievable at user workstations by means of graphical interface with the disk storage hardware. Use of the system in the Senate Library has grown dramatically since installation of its workstation in 1991; the number of pages of documents and articles printed in 1992 was 11,000.

PLANNING, FUNDING, AND BUDGETING

Planning is conducted on a short-term and long-term basis by the librarian with the participation of the assistant librarian and the section heads. The formal mechanism for most planning is the annual report on the library, which is compiled at the end of each calendar year for the Secretary of the Senate. It includes a section on planning, where the objectives for the past year are reviewed and measured in terms of what has been achieved, and states the objectives for the coming year. In the course of the year, these objectives may be modified by unanticipated events or developments. For instance, the objective to purchase a reference set or a microform collection may be changed if the publisher or vendor does not meet a publication deadline as planned; or a new product may unexpectedly come on the market that is determined to be of such importance that another planned acquisition is deferred. In any case, planning is always closely coordinated with the Secretary's Office and effected within the constraints of the library's annual budget.

Funding for the library's operations is provided in the annual appropriations for the legislative branch. The appropriation runs for the fiscal year of the federal government beginning October 1 through the following September 30. The funding levels are authorized by the Senate Committee on Appropriations and approved by the full Senate when the legislative branch appropriations bill comes to the floor. As with all appropriations measures, the concurrence of the House must also be obtained, and the bill must be signed into law by the President. Funding levels are based on the budget requests submitted to the Appropriations Committee by the principal officers of the Congress: the Secretary of the Senate, the Clerk of the House of Representatives, the Architect of the Capitol, the Librarian of Congress, the Public Printer, and others.

The budgeting cycle for the library begins in August of each year, some 14 months before the fiscal year is to begin. The budget of the current fiscal year is reviewed, as are the objectives defined in the planning section of the latest annual report. These budgets and plans largely determine the level of the budget requests to be made, and they provide the basis of the accompanying justifications, which are submitted to the Assistant Secretary of the Senate.

The Assistant Secretary receives the budgets from the various department heads under the Secretary of the Senate and coordinates them to develop a comprehensive budget of expenses for the entire Secretary's Office; also included in it is a separate account for staff salaries.

This comprehensive budget is reviewed by the Secretary of the Senate and presented in February or March of each year to the Legislative Branch Subcommittee of the Appropriations Committee. The full committee makes the determinations of spending levels for the entire Senate and reports its recommendations to the Senate, usually during the summer months. Legislative action on the appropriations bill is supposed to be completed before the end of September (though funding is otherwise provided on a temporary basis by means of a continuing resolution if this deadline is missed). Once the measure is enacted into law, the funds for the fiscal year become available.

The library's budget for services and materials consists of seven accounts, for which the Appropriations Committee authorized the following requested amounts in Fiscal Year 1994 (FY94):

Online information services	$ 69,200
Microform publications	36,000
Books	17,000
Subscriptions	23,000
Standing orders	22,000
CD-ROM products	4,000
Audio/visual materials	500
Total	$ 171,700

This total represents 12.5 percent of the amount authorized by the committee for the expenses of the Office of the Secretary. It is possible under restricted circumstances to transfer money from one account to another, but it is done only with proper justification. In addition to these accounts, the library will receive in FY94 a separate allocation of the Secretary's budget totalling $11,600 for stationery and office supplies, for travel and training, and for book preservation.

As costs for services and materials are incurred, they are paid for by means of a voucher system. Upon receipt of an invoice, the library's secretary prepares a voucher for payment, which is examined and signed by the librarian and by the Secretary of the Senate. Such vouchers are further reviewed by the auditing section of the Senate Disbursing Office and by the Senate Committee on Rules and Administration. After this process is completed, the Disbursing Office prepares checks for vendors and publishers, and issues payment.

Salaries for the library are included in the Secretary of the Senate's salary budget; in FY94 the library's allocation is estimated at almost $861,500 (about 7 percent of the total amount appropriated for the Secretary's Office). Over half this amount ($484,000) goes to professional staff salaries, the remainder to nonprofessional.

MARKETING

The library's efforts to promote awareness of its services among its user community are directed to three areas. The first is an outreach program that involves participation in a series of seminars jointly cosponsored by the Offices of the Secretary and of the Sergeant at Arms. These seminars are intended as orientation for new staff and strive to acquaint them with the range of services and facilities available to them throughout the Senate. There are, for example, classes in the use of computer systems, and seminars on the legislative process, Senate history, legal research, management techniques, and other topics.

The seminar on the services of the Senate Library is held three or four times each year. The event is advertised, and advance registration is requested. The seminar is attended by 25-30 people and lasts an hour and a half; it features an introduction to the library, demonstrations on database systems, and a tour of the facility.

Informal tours for an individual office are also arranged on request; they are briefer and less elaborate than the seminar format. In addition, the reference librarians give talks about the services of the Senate Library to Senate staff attending the CRS-sponsored District/State Institute seminar series and its orientation seminars for new Congressional staff.

The second area of marketing consists of a publication program. In years past the library published as many as half a dozen publications on various subjects–Senate election laws, Senate expulsion and censure cases, resolutions of amendments to the constitution, and presidential vetoes to list a few. The library has gradually ceased producing most of the publications that it used to compile. Its current major undertaking is the record of vetoes exercised by Presidents on legislation passed by the Congress, entitled *Presidential Vetoes, 1789-1991*.

Another useful publication compiled by the library's reference staff began as an internal tool and is now used as a promotional device as well. This publication is the *United States Senate Library Resources Directory*, a listing of legislative and legal materials, magazines, newspapers, wire services, and databases available in the library; it also includes useful reference materials and selected sets of government publications. Its particular utility is that each title entry is detailed by Senate Library holdings (either microform or paper copy), online availability, and specific database source. A third publication is the color brochure on library services, and operations; this pamphlet is a popular handout item.

The third area of promotion is the mailing of informational items from the library to Senate offices. The *Resources Directory* and the brochure are mailed to all newly elected Senators' offices at the beginning of each new Congress as well as to seminar participants. Another mailing is a list of currently pending legislation of timely interest, known as the *Hot Bills List*. It is compiled by the staff of the LEGIS section and sent out on a weekly basis to Senate offices that request it; 135 offices are currently receiving the list.

STATISTICAL INFORMATION

Sponsor: United States Senate

Name of Unit: Senate Library

Location: S-332, The Capitol
Washington, DC 20510

Name of Head of Unit: Roger K. Haley

Title of Head of Unit: Senate Librarian

Title of Immediate Supervisor: Secretary of the Senate

Staff Size: 10 professionals; 13 non-professionals

Main Subjects Collected: Legislation, Government, Politics, History, Biography

Collection Size:

Books:	55,000
Current subscriptions:	200
Bound journal volumes:	10 titles
Microfilm:	6,000 reels
Microfiche:	1,000,000
Clippings:	20 file drawers

Special Collections: Bills and Resolutions, Congressional hearings and debates, U.S. Congressional Serial Set

Computer Services: Burelle's, DataTimes, LEGI-SLATE, LEXIS, NEXIS, WESTLAW, Wilsonline, Senate LEGIS, SCORPIO (Library of Congress)

Number of Users: 7,000
(FY1993)

Area of Unit: 9,000 sq. ft.

Number of Seats for Users: 20

PART II:
JUDICIAL BRANCH

Chapter 2

Sixth Circuit Library for the United States Courts

Kathy Joyce Welker

The organizational structure of the federal judicial library system is directly linked to the organizational structure of the judiciary itself. That is, apart from the U.S. Supreme Court, the general jurisdiction federal court system is composed exclusively of twelve separate circuit courts of appeals, each with jurisdiction over a geographically defined region of the country. Each of these circuit courts of appeals, in turn, has its own circuit court library system.

One of these 12 library systems is the Sixth Circuit Library for the U.S. Courts, headquartered in Cincinnati, Ohio in the Potter Stewart Building. This library serves the U.S. Court of Appeals for the Sixth Circuit, which is the federal appellate court with general jurisdiction over the states of Kentucky, Michigan, Ohio, and Tennessee. This chapter describes the national court library program, in general, and the Sixth Circuit Library System, specifically. It should be carefully noted throughout, however, that the Sixth Circuit Library System is only one example of the widely divergent libraries located in the 12 circuit library systems.

If there is one constant principle that would lead to some understanding of the organization and management of the circuit library systems, it is that each system is unique. Each circuit has very different court and library histories, organizational structures, policies, and management patterns. Principles of judicial autonomy in decision making carry over into the process of managing and organizing circuit operations, including circuit libraries.

FEATURES COMMON TO ALL CIRCUIT LIBRARIES

Certain management elements are common to all of the circuits. These are directly related to statutory requirements and to actions of the Judicial Conference of the United States, the governing body of the federal judiciary.

Statutory requirements relating to circuit libraries are very few. To begin with, each circuit librarian is appointed by his or her court of appeals, and the circuit librarian (with the approval of the court) appoints his or her assistants.[1] The number of assistants that can be appointed is limited to the number of library positions allotted to each circuit by the Director of the Administrative Office of the U.S. Courts.[2] Additional statutory guidance may also be found in annual appropriations laws that fund the court library systems.

The Judicial Conference of the United States sets national policy for the judiciary. The Chief Justice of the Supreme Court presides over the judicial conference. Membership is composed of the chief judges of every court of appeals plus one district judge from each circuit court of appeals. Judicial conference (i.e., national) policies can be found in the *Guide to Judiciary Policies and Procedures*.[3]

Working with the Judicial Conference of the United States to both formulate and implement policy is the Administrative Office of the United States Courts. This office, located in Washington D.C., contains several divisions that impact library operations. The program office charged with guiding and supporting the national development of the court libraries is the Legal Research and Library Branch[4] (currently located in the Article III Judges Division). Other Administrative Office units with continual and major impact on library operations include the Lawbook Section, the Human Resources Division, the Space and Facilities Division, the Integrated Technology Division, and the Budget Division.

NATIONAL LIBRARY PROGRAM IMPLICATIONS

The establishment of a Legal Research and Library Program office (LRLB) in the Administrative Office (AO) of the U.S. Courts[5] in 1978 signaled to the judiciary that support and improve-

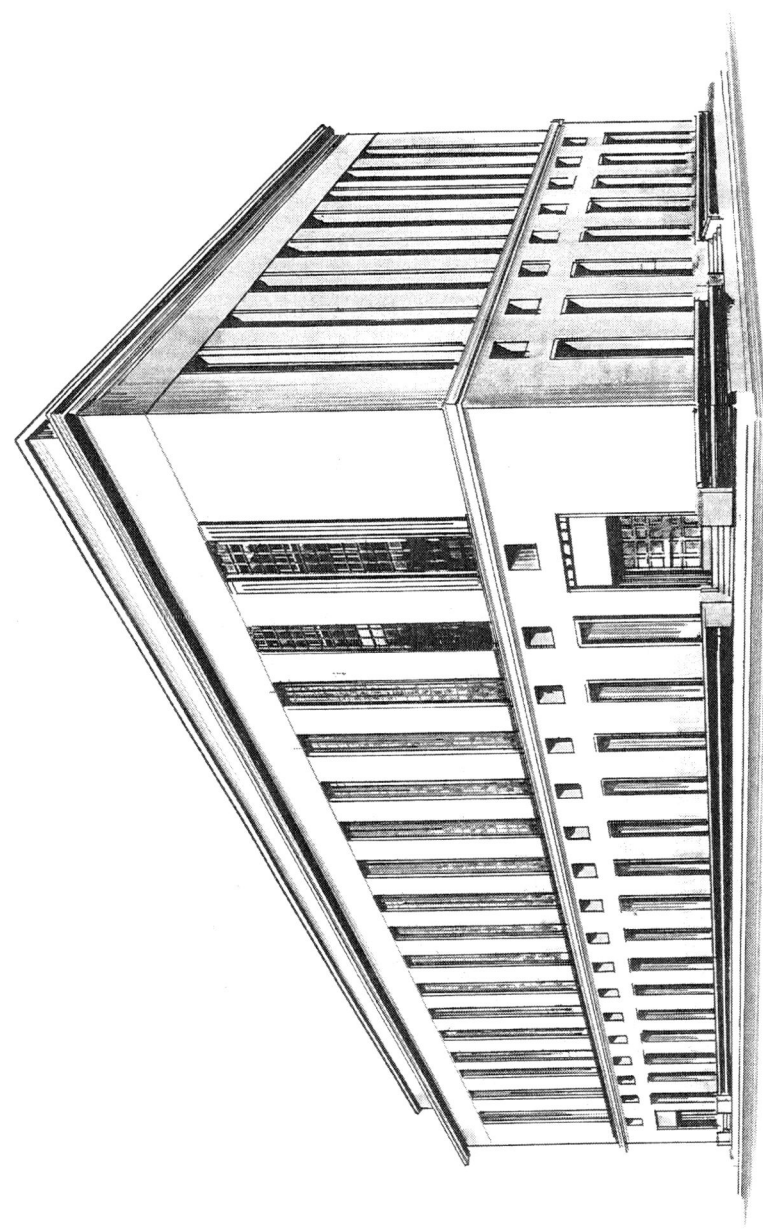

Photo 2.1. The newly dedicated Potter Stewart Building (formerly U.S. Post Office and Courthouse). Courtesy of Tim Hinton, General Services Administration.

ment of court libraries was a national priority. Concurrent with this establishment was the decision that court libraries would be organized as parts of circuit courts of appeals but would directly serve judges and other court personnel in all courts found within the geographical boundary of that circuit. This would include trial courts (known as U.S. District Courts) and U.S. Bankruptcy Courts in addition to the court of appeals. Libraries serving all of these courts would be part of one circuit system, not separately administered or funded units within the circuit and district courts.

It was also determined at this juncture that the number of library staff positions given to any particular circuit would be directly related to the number of judges served in that circuit. The total number of judges served (including circuit judges, district judges, bankruptcy judges, and magistrate judges) would determine how many library staff could be hired. The circuit could then determine where these staff would be located. For example, staff could be spread through the circuit in multiple branch library locations (most frequently called "satellite" libraries in the federal judiciary),[6] or they could be located at the main (or headquarters) location of the circuit, or in some combination of these locations.

The other limitation on the location of libraries and library staff was that every satellite must serve a minimum number of judges before it could be established and funded. Although the minimum number of judges that must be served by a satellite has changed over the years, the principle has remained that a minimum number is required.

A major component of the guidance and support provided by the AO to the Circuit Libraries is negotiating national prices and contracts for procurement purposes. Such procurements range from CALR (computer-assisted legal reference) services to lawbooks to computers (hardware and software).

CALR services have always been an integral part of the provision of library and legal research services to the judiciary. Primary providers of this service are both the LEXIS and WESTLAW legal research databases. A national contract negotiated by LRLB with the vendors who provide these services sets pricing structures, training requirements, user restrictions, etc. Under LRLB's direction, circuit library personnel administer the implementation of the judiciary's obligations under this CALR contract. These obligations extend to wherever CALR services are accessed in the judiciary, whether in libraries or in judges chambers or even in the homes of court personnel (wherever the judiciary is paying for that access).

The LRLB also contracts for access to other types of library specific databases. Through membership in FEDLINK,[7] the courts subscribe to such services as DIALOG and OCLC (Online Computer Library Center).[8] Uses of OCLC include bibliographic verification, extensive retrospective and current cataloging, and interlibrary loan network use. These database services have contributed greatly to providing access to information far beyond the boundaries of these circuit library operations.

Another national initiative plans to locate and implement an integrated library system for all of the circuit libraries. LRLB is staffing this process. The goal is to have in place an integrated library acquisitions, cataloging, and serials control system accessible by court personnel through the courts' wide area network. It is anticipated that this implementation may be phased in over a number of years.

NATIONAL LAWBOOK ORDERING IMPLICATIONS

The procurement of research materials (in whatever form of media) for the federal judiciary, to be placed in library and nonlibrary locations, is handled jointly by the AO and the circuit libraries. Through an evolutionary process, the role of libraries and library staff has increasingly become central to this process. When the library program was first established, purchasing and providing supplementation to published research materials (primarily lawbook materials) to the judiciary was done by the AO's Lawbook Section. An exception to this general rule was that many federal court libraries which predated the establishment of the library program had "local library funds" derived from local attorney admission fees. These local funds were also used to purchase published materials for local libraries. In a number of instances, these dual systems for library materials purchasing continue to this day.

As the judiciary exploded in size and as library personnel became increasingly knowledgeable and experienced in federal government materials purchasing, circuit library personnel began to actively participate in the ordering process. Bibliographic and price verification shifted from the AO to the libraries. In some circuits, library staff actually accessed the AO lawbook computer system and prepared purchase orders online as if they were Lawbook Section personnel. In addition, funds for new purchases for libraries and for nonlibrary locations were divided out to all the circuits instead of being held centrally at the AO.

The next step currently in process will make it possible for the circuits who wish to do so to order and renew research materials directly from the vendors, eliminating the need to funnel this process through the Lawbook Section. Money for this purpose will also be divided up and given to each circuit library system that elects to participate in this change. For these circuits, the main role for the AO will be to negotiate, on behalf of the judiciary, favorable price structures with the vendors who supply heavily used research materials. The AO may also oversee the procurement process in all of the circuits to assure that federal procurement regulations are followed.

NATIONAL PERSONNEL POLICIES

Since the judiciary is a separate branch of government from the executive and legislative branches, the Judicial Conference determines which elements of federal service policies will apply to judiciary employees. Judiciary employees are not part of civil service but rather serve "at the pleasure" of the judges.

Judiciary employees are placed on a pay schedule very similar to the general schedule for civil service employees, although job requirements and qualifications for the same pay in other branches will not necessarily match those established for judiciary employees. Pay for library employees is related to the placement of library personnel in the overall judiciary pay hierarchy of court positions. The placement of these positions in the court hierarchy has a very long history, although the relationship of pay rates to work being performed has been evolving over recent years. Librarians (who are professionally trained personnel) are relatively new to the judiciary pay system and are still being studied for appropriate placement in the overall court pay hierarchy.

In addition to pay scales, many other elements of personnel administration are determined nationally. Benefit packages are basically the same as those provided to civil service employees. Such elements as promotion criteria, waiting periods between pay grades, and amount of vacation and sick time tend to mirror those found in other branches of the government. Who has appointing (and firing) authority is also set nationally by statute or by the Judicial Conference for all court personnel, including library staffs.

Generally, changes to a myriad of national personnel policies affecting libraries must be approved on an item by item basis by the Judicial Conference of the United States. Interpretation of national personnel policies and development of policy changes is provided by the AO's Human Resources Division.

SPACE DESIGN AND MANAGEMENT

The landlord for the federal judiciary is the General Services Administration (GSA).[9] Construction and renovation of court facilities including libraries are either supplied by GSA or contracted for by GSA. GSA also contracts for maintenance and cleaning services, setting the terms of performance.

When court library space is being developed for occupation or for renovation, the *U.S. Courts Design Guide*[10] governs such considerations as amount of usable square footage allowable, or specific design elements such as lighting patterns, wiring for computers, sizes of individual offices, etc. The *U.S. Courts Design Guide* has been approved by the Judicial Conference of the United States, and any changes to it must also be approved by the conference.

NATIONAL AUTOMATION INITIATIVES

Automation policies are determined through the Integrated Technology Division (ITD)[11] of the AO. As court demands for computer hardware and software grew and because the financial ability to meet these demands was inadequate, the AO established an office to phase in and coordinate the installation of automation hardware and software. In addition to meeting this need, ITD has also developed national software programs that can automate processes common to many courts nationwide. Like all other units of the courts, libraries need such automation support, and their specific automation needs are fit into the overall hierarchy of court automation needs. Libraries are put into the queue for receiving necessary equipment and off-the-shelf software, and for the development of national customized software applications, as necessary.

CENTRALIZED VS. DECENTRALIZED BUDGETING IMPLICATIONS

Over a three-year period, the courts have "decentralized" the budgeting process to local courts and local court units, including circuit courts and circuit library systems. This process has given circuit libraries new flexibility in moving funds from one budget account to another as needs and requirements change. Decentralized budgeting allows a court unit (such as a library) flexibility in setting and implementing changing management goals. For example, if a library can operate with fewer personnel than is budgeted to that library, those personnel funds can be used to purchase needed computer equipment or books. Within certain limitations, such management decisions are left to the unit executive, that is the Circuit Librarian.

Local courts decide which budget accounts will be administered by local units (such as libraries) and which accounts will be administered centrally for the entire court. Courts also decide which unit of the court will administer each court-wide account for all of the units. For example, automation accounts may be administered for the entire court by the automation unit of the court or each court unit (such as the Clerk's Office, Staff Attorneys' Office and Library) may administer its own separate automation accounts. Or some of the automation accounts may be administered centrally while others may be administered within various units of the courts. The decisions made by the court regarding administration of certain budget accounts has a direct impact on the flexibility which each unit will have in transferring funds between accounts, and will directly affect how creative circuit library managers across the country can be in managing accounts and expenditures.

SIXTH CIRCUIT LIBRARY SYSTEM

Taking into consideration the overlay of national programs described above, let us now turn to a description of one specific circuit library system. The Sixth Circuit Library System itself is comprised of a main library in Cincinnati and seven branch libraries located in Cleveland, Columbus, Detroit, Grand Rapids, Memphis, Nashville, and Toledo. Two additional branches will open in the near future in Louisville and Chattanooga.

The circuit library system cannot be fully described merely by enumerating where each staffed library is located. More accurately the system is located wherever court personnel do business within the geographical boundaries of the four-state circuit. The personnel located in any one of more than forty towns or cities containing places of holding court or judicial chambers call upon the library system to provide legal research support services. Another measurement is that the library system provides purchasing and subscription maintenance support for over 300 separate mailing addresses throughout the circuit. At each of these locations, books and other published materials, and CALR services are provided in support of the courts' legal research needs.

HISTORY OF LIBRARY SYSTEM

The provision of these legal support services has been almost one hundred years in the making. It began with the establishment of the Sixth Circuit Library in Cincinnati in 1895.[12] The first record of a librarian being appointed is in 1898.[13] Throughout its history, this Cincinnati library has served the circuit court of appeals and the practicing bar of that court.

The first 80 years were times of slow growth. By the late 1970s, the Cincinnati Library staff consisted of only the circuit librarian and two technician assistants. It was very early in the 1980s that the library's mission changed dramatically. This change was precipitated by the fact that money was supplied by Congress to the courts of appeals to establish additional branch libraries. At the same time, no separately governed libraries could be established in district courts. In other words, funding would only be provided for regional systems of libraries organized along the same lines as the circuits themselves. Each circuit was given the authority and the funds to establish its own library system, which was expected to serve all court personnel within that circuit.

So it was early in 1981 that the circuit librarian became responsible for supervising a remote library, that is, the library serving the U.S. District Court in Detroit. The Detroit library was a one-person library with a librarian in charge who now was expected to report to the Circuit Librarian in Cincinnati. As a result, the Detroit library became the first branch of the Sixth Circuit Library System, and the mission of the district library in Detroit was redefined to serve all court personnel located in Detroit whether they worked for the circuit, district, or bankruptcy court.

After that, changes came rapidly. By 1985, branches in Nashville (1981), Memphis (1983), Grand Rapids (1983), and Cleveland (1985) had been established, each with a professionally trained librarian in charge. Two more branches in Columbus (1989) and Toledo (1990) were opened and staffed much more recently. Two additional branches in Chattanooga (1995) and Louisville (1994) will be opened and staffed. Each of the existing branch libraries has a full-time professional librarian plus at least one part-time library technician to assist.

During the same time period, the Cincinnati staff grew very quickly to nine positions. This library had become the headquarters of a series of remote branches as well as the service point for dozens of locations unserved by any branch library. The Cincinnati collection grew in order to support the book needs of court personnel numbering in the hundreds. The space occupied by the library tripled in 1988 and the staff size also multiplied.

Services initiated from Cincinnati were numerous. Library collections in all locations were cataloged for the first time. Ordering was initiated for the over 300 locations where book collections are found throughout the circuit. Circuit-wide coordination of interlibrary loan, reference, CALR, and systems services was put into place. Standardization of personnel and budget practices was generally accomplished. Space designs were developed, and construction oversight was provided for remote satellite libraries. The overall operational role of Cincinnati library staff became the support of branch libraries so that branch staff could concentrate on their primary duty and responsibility of providing efficient and accurate reference and research support services to the judges in the circuit. The provision of all of these new services came about concurrently with the development of a much more expansive understanding of the role and mission of the circuit library.

CIRCUIT LIBRARY MISSION

The mission of the library system is to provide general and legal research support services to all of the federal courts within the geographical boundaries of the four states comprising the Sixth Circuit. Individual branch libraries are responsible for providing primary service to all judges located within the boundaries of the district where that library is located. (One of the more populous districts, Northern District of Ohio, is actually served by two branch libraries in Cleveland and Toledo.) In districts where no branch library is located, judges there are primarily served by the Cincinnati library. It is the overall plan that there will be in time a branch library established in every district of the circuit with the possible exception of the Eastern District of Kentucky, which is located very close to Cincinnati and can generally be served from there.

COURT(S) SERVED BY LIBRARY SYSTEM

The Sixth Circuit Library System is an administrative unit of the U.S. Court of Appeals for the Sixth Circuit, whose main offices are located in Cincinnati; circuit judges have their resident chambers in 14 cities and towns found throughout and within the geographical boundaries of the circuit. The judges travel to Cincinnati to hear cases as part of three-judge panels a number of times each year.

Circuit court policy is set by the Chief Circuit Judge and by the 15 active judges of the court. Reporting to the judges is the court's senior staff, which includes the Circuit Executive, the Clerk of Court, the Senior Staff Attorney, and the Circuit Librarian.

Unlike some other units of the Sixth Circuit, the circuit library system also serves all of the lower courts that are located within the geographical boundaries of the circuit. These lower courts include nine trial courts (called U.S. District Courts), and nine bankruptcy courts. When all of the judges in these courts are added to the number serving in the circuit court, the total is 190 (as of January 1, 1995).

LIBRARY COMMITTEES AND LIBRARY JUDGES

Because the number of judges served is so large and widespread geographically, there is a system of library advisory committees in place to work with the Circuit Librarian. A number of separate library committees exist throughout the Sixth Circuit. These local committees (including a Court of Appeals Library Committee) may consist of a group of judges, but more commonly is just one "library judge." The committee or judge is available to advise librarians on policy matters regarding local libraries. In addition, the Circuit Librarian consults with local committee members or the library judge when evaluating the performance of branch librarians and when formulating policy affecting that particular local library.

There is also a circuit-wide library committee (called the Circuit Advisory Committee on Libraries) which meets with the Circuit Librarian on an annual basis at the Sixth Circuit Judicial Conference to review the operation of the library system over the previous year, and to raise questions and concerns about library policy issues. The circuit-wide committee consists of the chair of the Court of Appeals Library Committee (who also serves as chair of the circuit-wide committee) and a library judge from each of the branch library locations. Librarians actively encourage the courts to designate library committee members or library judges.

ORGANIZATIONAL AND REPORTING RELATIONSHIPS

The judges of the appeals and district courts are "Article III"[14] judges. They are appointed by the President and have life tenure.

Chief judges of these courts are determined by seniority on the bench and their tenure as chief judge is limited to seven years.

The circuit librarian is appointed by the court of appeals and is subject to removal by that court.[15] In turn, the circuit librarian appoints "library assistants" in numbers funded by the Administrative Office of the U.S. Courts.[16] All "library assistants" are hired, fired, and evaluated by the circuit librarian (with the approval of the circuit court). These library assistants range from the Deputy Circuit Librarian to branch librarians to library technicians.

Because the Judicial Conference of the United States has not addressed many specific personnel issues, this is often left to the courts themselves. In lieu of judges of the court setting these specific personnel policies, this responsibility is often further delegated to members of the court's senior staff as a group, or to the individual unit executives, of which the circuit librarian is one. Therefore, it generally falls to the circuit librarian to set personnel policies that the court will deem appropriate.

The very flat organizational structure of the entire judiciary (as demonstrated by the general independence of individual courts) is mimicked in the organizational structure of the Sixth Circuit Library System. No district court is above another; each operates independently of another. Branch libraries serving generally autonomous courts (that is, districts) function parallel to, but in some ways, independent of each other. At the same time, branch libraries answer to Cincinnati staff on matters related to defined functional areas.

A diagram illustration of this organizational structure can be found in the chart at the end of this article. This chart illustrates the fact that circuit-wide service functions are coordinated and/or supervised from Cincinnati. These functions include administration (such as personnel, systems, and budget administration), acquisitions, database access, interlibrary loan support, and cataloging.

Cincinnati staff with these functional responsibilities operate in a matrix-type supervisory relationship to the rest of the Cincinnati staff and to the branches. Within their defined areas of functional responsibility, they set the policies governing applications and procedures that must be followed by all library staff. For example, it is the responsibility of the cataloger to define and supervise all cataloging activities both in Cincinnati and in all of the branches.

The organizational chart also demonstrates another practical limit inherent in the library system that results in a great deal of autonomy in branch libraries. The sheer number of satellites (nine) supervised by the Circuit and Deputy Circuit Librarians makes it impossible to supervise activities closely. Added to that the fact is that most of these branches are hundreds of miles from the main library and that travel funds are very limited; staff in branch libraries must work out their own ways to support local courts. One could never accuse the circuit library system of having redundant layers of middle managers or an organizational structure that is too vertically layered!

Because branch librarians are located in remote locations away from the Cincinnati library, they must have wide discretion as to how the work is organized and performed there. It is up to the satellite librarians to assess how best to provide research and library services to their local courts. They must independently deliver the library services required by judges and other court staff in their location while still using other branch librarians and the Cincinnati library as advisors and as suppliers of support services.

This organizational arrangement underscores the need for highly competent and professionally trained librarians in every one of the branch libraries. These librarians must have a certain level of skill, ability, and self-confidence that allows them to gain the respect of their local courts for their research capabilities. It is these abilities that lead judges and other court personnel to rely upon the services which a good legal research library can provide.

MANAGING IN A DECENTRALIZED ENVIRONMENT

The major challenge inherent in managing a system of libraries serving the courts is that the entire organizational structure is highly decentralized. This is not a "top-down" organization. Since it can more correctly be described as generally decentralized, each court (whether it is a circuit, district, or bankruptcy court) operates very independently of other courts.

Local variation is the norm. Circumstances and individualized modes of decision making have worked together to create widely divergent ways of doing business in every individual court. As in the law itself, local precedent can be determinative when local policy issues are considered.

Because librarians work as an integral part of the opinion formulation process, the way they do business (that is, deliver services) is a matter of great concern to local judges. Judges are the clients of the library services; therefore, their interests and support are of utmost concern to the librarians who serve them. In the delivery of research and reference services, only the judges and their staffs are the evaluators of service quality. The input of these judges is actively sought by librarians at every juncture when policy is formulated so that the provision of a quality end product is always held up as the standard for measuring success.

This local policy formulation for a satellite occurs in a number of areas. Particularly when setting circulation policies, and determining collection development needs, each local library has its own unique policies. These policies are determined by a number of factors such as the library's unique history, proximity, and accessibility to other local law library services, local security concerns, and the court (e.g., trial vs. appellate) primarily served in that location.

In contrast, system-wide policy formulation is most common in areas of personnel administration and in establishing standardized procedures for the provision of central services from the main library, such as book ordering and cataloging. Because local variations must be carefully considered, the formulation of system-wide policy often results from the work of an ad hoc committee of main and branch librarians who develop a draft policy for consideration and adoption by the circuit librarian.

The challenge to library managers in such a system is to be able to work in an environment replete with certain ambiguities. System-wide imperatives must be constantly balanced with local needs. Often a policy question cannot be answered with a simple "yes" or "no" but rather with a definite "maybe" depending on which of the libraries is affected by the policy statement.

CONCLUSION

A federal judicial library is administered as an integral part of the courts it serves. With an overlay of somewhat complex national priorities, circuit library systems get their marching orders from the judges who are also their clients. The Sixth Circuit Library System is one example of how a circuit system has been uniquely developed to provide legal research support services to its own judges and courts.

NOTES

1. 28 U.S.C. 713 (Supp. 1992)
2. Ibid.
3. *Guide to Judiciary Policies and Procedures*, (Washington, DC: Administrative Office of the U.S. Courts, 1977-).
4. Hereinafter referred to as LRLB.
5. Hereinafter referred to as AO.
6. Throughout this chapter, the terms "branch" and "satellite" libraries are used interchangeably.
7. FEDLINK is a cooperative program of FLICC (Federal Library and Information Center Committee) which was created by joint action of the Library of Congress and the Bureau of the Budget and which offers federal agencies opportunities to network resources.
8. Online Computer Library Center is located in Dublin, Ohio.
9. Hereinafter referred to as GSA.
10. *U.S. Courts Design Guide*, [3rd Ed.], (Washington, DC: Administrative Office of the U.S. Courts, Space and Facilities Division, 1991-).
11. Hereinafter referred to as ITD.
12. Frank O. Loveland, "In the Matter of the Library," *Journal: U.S. Circuit Court of Appeals, Sixth Circuit*, (Cincinnati: Dec. 12, 1900), 322.
13. *History of the Sixth Circuit*, (Cincinnati: Bicentennial Committee of the Judicial Conference of the United States, 1976), 30.
14. U.S. Constitution, Art. III.
15. 28 U.S.C. 713 (Supp. 1992).
16. Ibid.

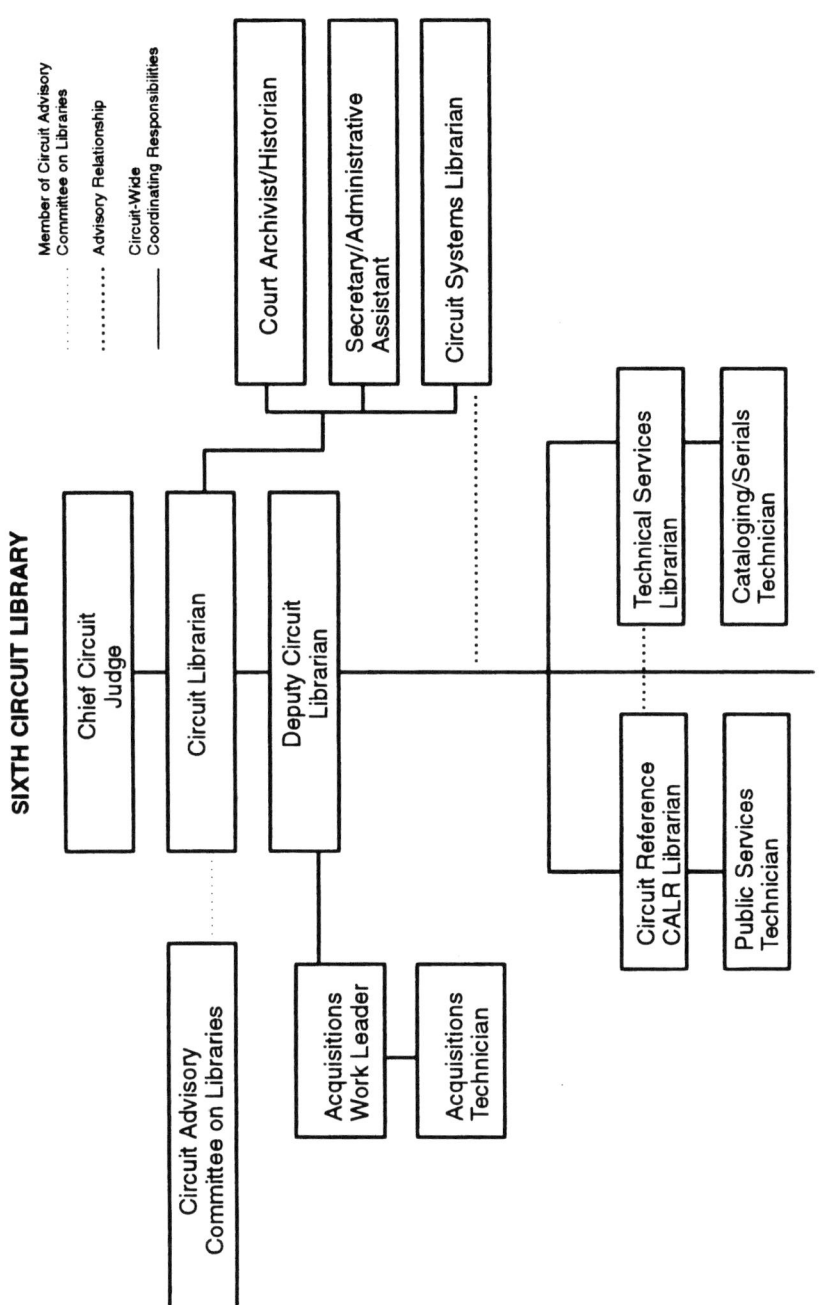

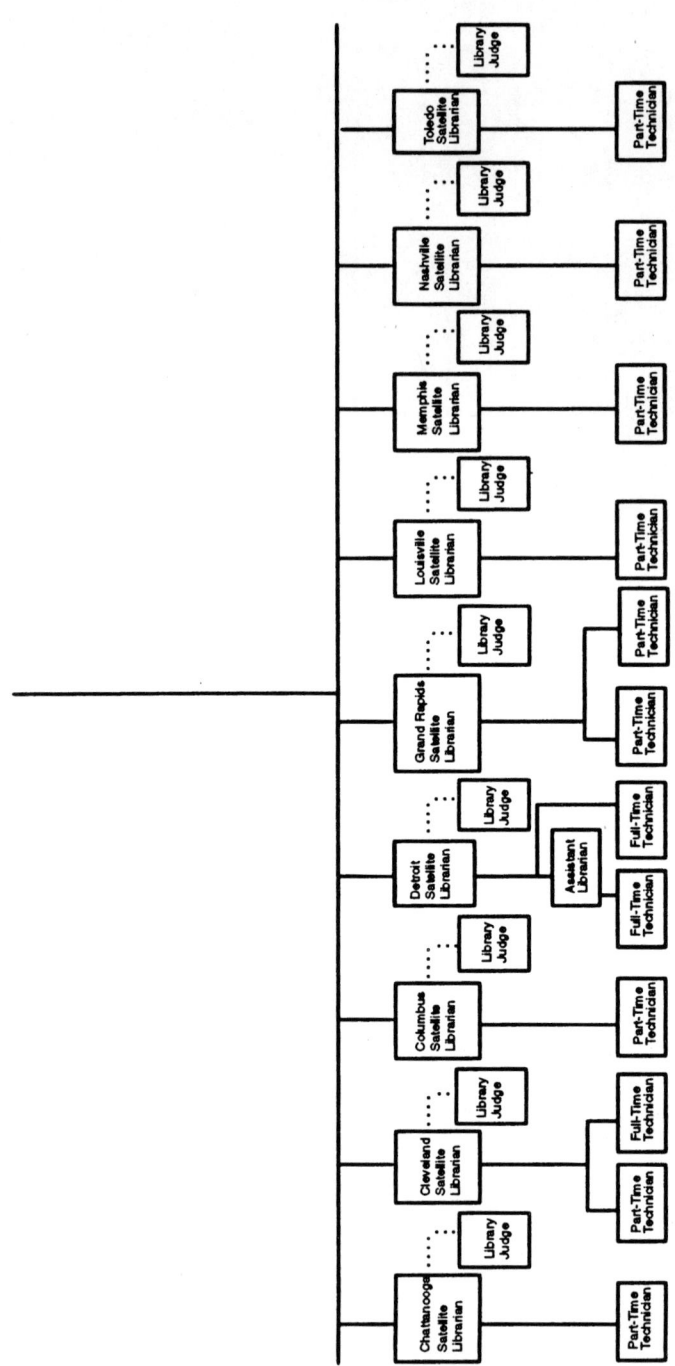

STATISTICAL INFORMATION

Sponsor:	Federal Judiciary
Name of Unit:	Sixth Circuit Library for the U.S. Courts
Location:	U.S. Post Office and Courthouse Building Cincinnati, Ohio 45202
Name of Head of Unit:	Kathy Joyce Welker
Title of Head of Unit:	Circuit Librarian
Title of Immediate Supervisor:	Chief Judge of the Sixth Circuit
Staff Size:	11 professionals; 15 non-professionals
Main Subjects Collected:	American Law
Collection Size:	
Books:	221,022 (including microfiche and reports)
Current subscriptions:	9,000
Special Collections:	Court History and Judicial Administration

Computer Services: LEXIS, WESTLAW, NEXIS, DIALOG, OCLC

Number of Users: 34,000, including 15,000 visitors
(FY1993)

Area of Unit: 16,000 sq. ft. (Cincinnati); 31,000 sq. ft. (7 branches)

Number of Seats for Users: 140 (Cincinnati and branches)

PART III:
EXECUTIVE BRANCH

Chapter 3

Department of Defense: Army Libraries

Louise Nyce

TYPES OF LIBRARIES

In the Executive Branch, the various services of the Department of Defense (Army, Air Force, Navy, Marine Corps) have libraries to support their primary mission–to provide for the defense of the United States through deterrence and, in the event of war, to fight to protect interests of the United States.

Within the individual services, all types of libraries are established and supported by their parent organizations to respond to the more defined organizational missions, e.g., combat development, training, research, development, test and evaluation, civil works, military construction, health services, legal, educational, and corporate information needs. As in other Federal Agencies, there is only one legally mandated departmental library, the Pentagon Library, but other libraries are established at Headquarters, major commands, installations, and activities. The library programs provide general reading materials whenever the military is deployed for missions outside the U.S. When the military is activated, libraries also play a significant role in fulfilling information needs, particularly in questions relating to the area involved and in mission support areas.

There are a few libraries, such as Army's Military History Institute, that have unique purposes. Although all libraries operate under the same basic professional standards, they do not all perform the same services, which are tailored to the specific needs defined by the library mission and the clientele served. Established libraries are normally under the direction of a professional librarian with a support staff of other librarians and library technicians. The staff selects, acquires, organizes, retrieves, disseminates, and evaluates information resources.

POLICY DIRECTION

Military libraries usually receive broad general policy direction from Headquarters, which is normally based on executive order, or federal law, and which reflect DoD's direction in carrying out the order. While many of the subordinate major commands or field operating agencies may supplement those directions, there is often great latitude on application in the individual library operation. In the various services, the placement of libraries within the organization is an important consideration since the support of the operation is often dependent upon the visibility and the contribution that an individual library makes to the performance of the mission.

COOPERATIVE EFFORTS

Although there is great commonality of issues in library operation among the services, there have been regrettably few instances of lasting cooperative efforts. These few instances are usually limited to a publication identifying special collections, (e.g., *A Census of Special Resources* developed by a task force group formed at a Military Librarian's Workshop, sponsored by Military Librarian's Division, Special Libraries Association), or through personal networking established by sharing experiences at other professional meetings. Military librarians also contribute their expertise and problem solving techniques to other organizations, such as ALA's Federal Librarian's Roundtable (FLRT), and the Armed Forces Librarian's Roundtable (AFLRT). Currently, military librarians are contributing members to the Federal Library and Information Center Committee (FLICC), and take leadership roles in many aspects of Federal Librarianship. These include being voting representatives to OCLC, or participating in national standards development through the National Institute of Standards and Technology (NIST), or as Chair of a FLICC committee to achieve revised classification and qualification standards from Office of Personnel Management, or by being named a representatives to the White House Conference of Libraries and Information Sciences. Military librarians are active on all levels, and comprise one-third of the Federal (Librarians) Workforce. (Source: OPM, *Occupational Federal and White Collar Workforce*, 1991.)

ARMY LIBRARY MANAGEMENT OFFICE

Of the three services, Army Libraries probably have the strongest cohesiveness and framework for their cooperation. In 1976, the Adjutant General authorized *Study of U.S. Army Libraries*, which concluded there was a need for a central organization to permit development of uniform directives and standards for support, technical guidance, and solutions to common library problems. In 1978 the Army Library Management Office (ALMO) was established with a staff of three persons; it was later placed under the Office of the Director of Information, Command, Control, Communications, and Computers (DISC4). Another recommendation of the 1976 study, the establishment of an Army Library Committee (ALC), was also implemented in 1978 with representatives from all major commands and all types of libraries. It was through this committee that many cooperative projects were sponsored: an Inter-Library Loan Directory, a guide paper on Getting Started in Library Automation, identification of Baseline Automation Requirements, training modules for Library Technicians (with video), and many "how to" projects and promotional materials publicizing library features.

ARMY LIBRARY INSTITUTE

The annual Army Library Institute training was also institutionalized and sponsored by the Army Library Committee to meet service-specific training needs. The Planning Board of the Army

Librarian Career Program contributed to the new structure for a competitive career referral program, complete with training plans, intern training requirements, and an assessment package. In 1993 the Army Library Listserv (ALL) was established for the Army Library Committee by the U.S. Military Academy, West Point, and is considered a vehicle for sharing information with other DoD Libraries.

ELECTRONIC GATEWAY TO ARMY LIBRARIES

Probably the most important cooperative effort is the Electronic Gateway to Army Libraries (EGAL) developed by librarian subject matter experts in 1992 through the Installation Support Management (ISM) initiative to connect data and information processes on an installation. When implemented, EGAL becomes a true link between, among, and beyond the libraries in that it connects all libraries, avoids search and display holding charges, and allows equal access to information, no matter the size or location of the library. It allows multiple searches using a single search strategy. EGAL differs from other gateways in that it also connects with installation data sources. It has potential as an intra-service link as well. EGAL continues to enjoy support and is scheduled to be implemented in the 1995-1997 time frame.

The following case studies reflect the experience of two large Army Libraries with different organizational missions and different customers. Comparable experiences may be found in the other services.

Chapter 4

The Pentagon Library

Louise Nyce

HISTORICAL DEVELOPMENT

The Pentagon Library is the second oldest Federal Library after the State Department Library. It has been reconstituted several times, and was designated the Departmental Library for the War Department (later Defense) a year after the Pentagon was built in 1943. A study made by Keyes Metcalf, then Director of Libraries at Harvard University, located some 23 libraries in the Pentagon and seven more War Department Libraries in the Washington area. He made the case for a single library focus, stating that the present situation is one of *uncoordinated decentralization*. There are too many libraries and a tendency to start additional ones on the slightest pretext. Subsequently, Secretary of War, George C. Marshall established the library to serve all the requirements in the Pentagon with the Army tasked to provide support. In 1983, it was renamed the Pentagon Library to more accurately reflect the mission to support the policy and decision makers in the Pentagon, and those in the National Capital Region not having formal libraries. (See Photos 4.1, 4.2, 4.3.)

MANAGER'S RESPONSIBILITIES

The Army has been tasked with providing Library and Information Services for all of the military/civilian components in the Pentagon. The Library is a Division of the United States Army Service Center for the Armed Forces, and is placed under the Administra-

Photo 4.1. Courtesy of Louise Nyce. Pentagon Library.

tive Assistant (AA) to the Secretary of the Army. The Library Director is responsible not only for the operation of the Library, but is called upon as a library subject matter expert in many projects, in staffing of policy actions, and in many cases becomes the AA's spokesperson on library matters. In this capacity, the director is the designated DoD representative to the Federal Library and Information Center Committee, and the representative to various boards and study groups (e.g., the FLICC Policy Working Group, and chair of the Personnel Working Group, where work on new classification/ qualification standards is ongoing.) As a Departmental Library, it has a special relationship with the Library of Congress, other national libraries, and comparable institutions.

LIBRARY PATRONS

The decision makers in the Pentagon are supported by what are called "action officers" (AO). Although famous and well-known people personally use the Pentagon Library, normally the back-

Photo 4.2. Courtesy of Louise Nyce. Pentagon Library.

ground research is performed by action officers who prepare decision papers or briefings based on their findings. The action officers are the Pentagon Library's primary customers, along with the historians, attorneys, speechwriters, study groups, researchers, the officer "students" or fellows, contractors, retirees, and all other persons who expect an answer or a referral because they don't know who else to call–even if it is from a phone booth in London. Increasingly, the organizations that are served are becoming "purple"–the color selected to represent the amalgamation of all of the services.

ACCESS POLICY

The basic access policy is that if you can get into the building, you can use the library. Entrance into the building is by official pass, issued to persons with official work or business with the Pentagon. Circulation of items, extensive (or expensive) searches are limited to the identified supported community. While official requests for visitors are received from foreign countries, there is a clearance process which

Photo 4.3. Courtesy of Louise Nyce. Pentagon Library.

requires significant lead time. The library is unable to provide escort service for visitors.

SCOPE OF THE COLLECTION

The subject matter interests of the action officers and other official users determine the composition of the collection and the selection of information resources. The library is probably best categorized as a research library with the general collection having an emphasis on military art/science/history/affairs, international relations, international and U.S. treaties, geopolitics and foreign area/country studies, political science, public policy and administration, current issues and events, congressional materials, and law, management, and computer sciences. Special collections are found in Military Studies (classified materials) and Military Documents, including current regulations as well as an historical collection of War Department, Army, and DoD administrative publications. The periodicals and microform collection is formidable, and the law collection has been called one of the best in town.

The library is not large by common standards (463,000 monographs/documents, 2500 journal subscriptions), and it seats 165, but size becomes less of a factor as we move into the information supermarket. A net interlibrary loan lender, the library is also a partial GPO (Government Printing Office) depository library. Adding to the difficulty of maintaining a current, relevant collection is the fact that there is a no-growth policy because of the constraints of size (27,000 sq. ft.) and physical layout. Collection development policies supplement but do not replace the foresight of the librarians who select materials and who know the world of their customers and the dynamics of change.

STAFFING AND ORGANIZATION

The staff has ranged from a high of 87 to a low of 34. When staff is sparse, attempts are made to effect a form of trio of priorities, both in services and in essential background work. The organizational structure is currently rather traditional, but undergoing re-evaluation as Defense pares down. There are two divisions–Research and Information Services (branches: General Reference, Law, Military Studies/ Documents, Periodicals, Circulation), and Technical Services (Acquisition and Cataloging). The Systems Librarian reports to the Director. The Technical Services division provides the drive to keep the collection current once the materials are selected, is accountable for all materials as property, and handles the bindery and acquisition-deacquisition processes.

The automated acquisition subsystem to Pentagon Library Users System (PLUS), now being tested, will integrate the tracking elements necessary for both the procurement and financial reporting elements. A staff of three handles personnel records, filing, mail, facility and financial management, correspondence, records, publications, and other administrative functions of the library. Low staffing levels are the most serious problem even as use is increasing. Currently there are two people in circulation trying to handle circulation and attendance each averaging over 1,200 a day.

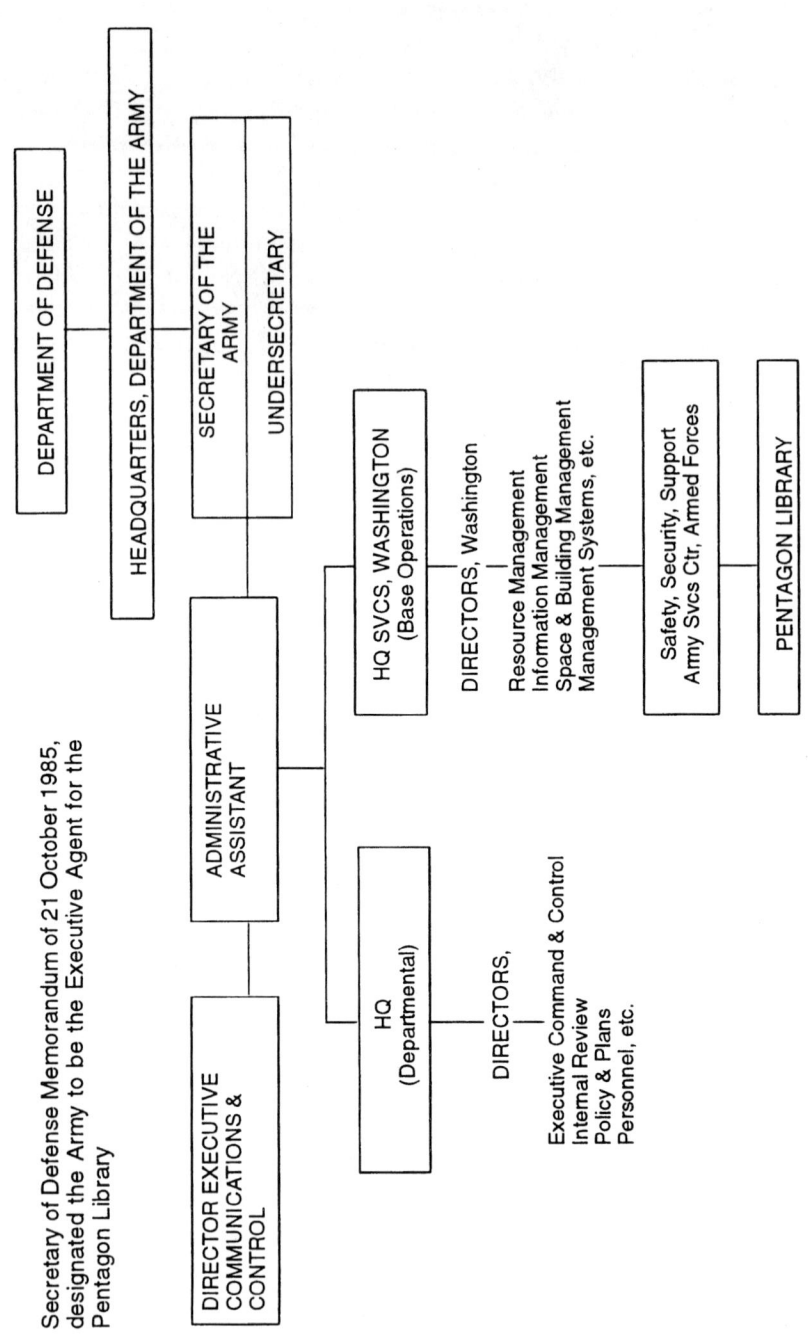

PENTAGON LIBRARY USERS SYSTEM

The engine of the Pentagon Library operation is its integrated library system known as PLUS (Pentagon Library Users System), a Unix-based reconstituted model of the ILS (Integrated Library System) which was a pioneer system developed with the National Library of Medicine in the 1970s. PLUS is the functional system through which circulation, serials, the public catalog, and bibliographic controls are managed. A CD-ROM local area network (LAN) with 84 drives is used for a variety of bibliographic, full-text, and statistical type databases.

CD-ROM PRODUCTS

The library has developed two CD-ROM products. The MILDOCS *on Disc* is a test prototype of military documents on disc designed to preserve this unique information in electronic format. Further funding is being pursued to continue this project. *Defense Library* on disc is a CD-ROM product which contains the unclassified union catalog holdings of the Pentagon Library, the National Defense University, and the Armed Forces Staff College holdings. Military periodical indexing and other military collections are planned additions. The disc is sold on a subscription basis through the National Technical Information Service (NTIS).

FISCAL SUPPORT

Fiscal support is projected on an annual basis, with both a baseline and a list of prioritized unfinanced requirements. Until recently, funding levels were relatively stable, and the important unfinanced requirements were supported during the year through transfer of monies from other entities not able to get approvals or otherwise use funds. Automation projects and cost projections are also developed annually, as are training needs. Spending is tracked and reported on a quarterly basis. As funding levels diminish, the issue of buying the same materials in several media becomes a concern, especially until the viability of CD-ROM products is assessed.

The task of keeping subscriptions renewed without interruption challenges the best management skills, particularly since so much of the procurement action is handled outside of the library and since release of funds can be delayed because of political processes (e.g., a Continuing Resolution when the Defense budget is not passed), or because of fluctuations in organizational priorities. The ability to acquire materials through the Federal Library and Information Center (FEDLINK) network for a service fee simplifies the process since the aggregate number of libraries using the FEDLINK contracts allows better pricing and is far more responsive in meeting a timeliness factor than when processed by each individual procurement office.

TRAINING AND TOURS

How well a library operates eventually comes back to the quality of the staff–the excellence of their background, the relevancy and currency of their training, their professionalism and commitment, and their ability to see the operation as a whole–the sum of its parts. The Washington, DC location has greatly improved the ability to provide updated training for the staff. But the staff also trains others. Each year six to eight librarian interns each spend a month at the Pentagon library, and it sponsors a month-long competitive developmental assignment on networking for three to four experienced Army Librarians.

The staff also sponsors one day of the Catholic University's annual Institute on Federal Library Resources, conducts numerous tours for a variety of groups, and consults with other individuals on library procedures and experiences. The staff develops bibliographies and fact sheets on issues and library operations. One notable example is the *Military References and Resources* which was used for training sessions at two Army Library Institutes. Individuals on the staff are frequently invited to speak at meetings, and are active members of professional organizations, many holding office. The staff is the glue that defines the concept of information services, which is the business of the Pentagon Library.

STATISTICAL INFORMATION

Sponsor: Department of Defense, Office of Secretary of the Army

Name of Unit: Pentagon Library and Information Services

Location: The Pentagon Washington, DC 20310-6605

Name of Head of Unit: Louise Nyce

Title of Head of Unit: Director

Title of Iimmediate Supervisor: Administrative Assistant to Secretary of the Army

Staff Size: 17 professionals; 26 non-professionals

Main Subjects Collected: Military Arts/Science/History/Technical Reports/Documents; Public Administration/Management; Political Science/Geopolitics; Country Studies/Economics/History; International Relations; Law, Congressional Materials/Documents; Contemporary Events; Computer Science/Information Management

Collection Size:

Books:	463,000
Current subscriptions:	2,094
Bound journal volumes:	12,545
Pamphlets, reports, audio-visual, etc.:	14,186

Special Collections: DOD/DA Administrative Documents; Law

Computer Services: BRS, DIALOG, DMS, DTIC DROLS, DUNSPRINT, LEGI-SLATE, LEXIS, NEXIS, MATRIS, OCLC, USNI PRESS/PERISCOPE, Washington Alert, WESTLAW

Number of Users: 237,709
(FY1993)

Area of Unit: 27,000 sq. ft.

Number of Seats for Users: 165

Chapter 5

Redstone Scientific Information Center (RSIC)

Sybil H. Bullock

BACKGROUND

Scientific and technical information is disseminated to scientists and engineers by two processes: formal and informal. The formal process relies on libraries/clearinghouses, librarians/technical information specialists, information products (journals, technical reports, etc) and services, and information storage and retrieval systems. The informal process relies on collegial contacts such as peers, coworkers, colleagues, gatekeepers, and consultants. Both processes are necessary for effective utilization of scientific and technical information. The Redstone Scientific Information Center (RSIC) relies on both processes for dissemination of information.

Located on Redstone Arsenal in Huntsville, Alabama, RSIC is the Army's largest scientific and technical information center with more than four million items covering both open and closed literature. The entire Department of Defense (DoD) and NASA research and development collections in 45 subject areas from aeronautics to space technology are available along with internationally published material (books, journals, monographs) in science and technology. Material collected is available in both English and foreign languages, and an in-house translation staff is present to provide translations of scientific and technical information into English for customers. Customers are scientists and engineers working for Defense and NASA, either as government employees or contractors.

RSIC was established in the early 1960s by consolidating seven existing scientific and technical collections at Redstone Arsenal into one centralized research library (see Photo 5.1). A study performed by Jerrold Orne, Joseph Shipman, and Robert Vosper recommended "that a major, central research library be established to serve all agencies and to coordinate the total library effort," and "that a general library director of high academic and professional competence, imagination, and drive be appointed" to lead the development of this major research library (Orne, Shipman, and Vosper, 1961).

That study provided the foundation for the primary mission which is to provide, via an extensive scientific and technical collection, accurate, timely, relevant information and services needed by scientists and engineers at Marshall Space Flight Center and the Army Missile Command and their contractors. Recognizing that the greater the accessibility of the information, the greater the use by the scientists and engineers, RSIC has modeled its operations and services to be as accessible as possible within budget constraints.

Over the years this mission has expanded to supporting other Army and NASA installations, Navy and Air Force installations, National Laboratories engaged in Aerospace/Defense research, over 130 federal agencies and their government contractors, and over 140 colleges and universities performing research and development. This support is provided through interlibrary loans of materials and personal visits to RSIC by the customer needing the information. RSIC is a net lender of materials; over 12,000 items were loaned outside RSIC through interlibrary loans in 1993, whereas only 1,000 were borrowed by RSIC for its customers' use (Long, 1993). Remote access to the RSIC unclassified computer is available for use by selected customers (see Photo 5.2).

Since its inception, both the size and value of this collection to the nation's scientific community has grown. As a result, RSIC now serves, via electronic networks, technical users throughout the U.S. and the world.

PLANNING AND BUDGETING

Planning for resources needed to operate effectively includes both short-term and long-term planning. Short-term planning involves current and next year requirements and is done through the

Photo 5.1. Entrance to Redstone Scientific Information Center Multi-Agency Library located on Redstone Arsenal at Huntsville, Alabama. Courtesy of U.S. Army.

Photo 5.2. RSIC customers using specifications and standards on CD/ROM. Courtesy of U.S. Army.

budgeting process. Input for short-term planning is compiled through meetings with library staff where priorities are developed for requirements for materials, equipment, services, and personnel. Input is received from the customers through official data calls from the director, from surveys, from informal dialogue with "technological gatekeepers," and from informal conversations with staff.

Long-term planning utilizes the strategic plans developed by the agencies supported by RSIC and the needs of the RSIC customers. A five-year plan developed by the director, key staff members, and key scientists and engineers outlines the long-term planning process and is developed from information gathered in meetings and discussions. These meetings may be held in the library or off site. The finished product is an outline with priorities for RSIC to use as a guide for decision making in the area of resources (Redstone Scientific Information Center, 1988). It is flexible so that rapid changes in the scientific and information technology world can be acknowledged.

The projected five-year plan for 1994-1998 is currently being developed. Problems exacerbating the planning process include the rapid expansion of scientific and technical information, and its corresponding increase in cost, and the rapidly changing information technology world. Decisions on day to day purchases are made by library staff with input from the customers. Customers who interface with the library staff include identified information linkers or gatekeepers in each research directorate.

RSIC is governed by an eight-member board with members from both NASA and Army. Chairmanship of the Board rotates between NASA and the Army, and the Board meets annually to review and approve the yearly budget, and provide information and input to the director for new/revised programs. The five-year plan provides the Board with information to determine large expenditures that may need to be programmed in the future, for example, computer enhancements, modifications to buildings, or large shelving purchases. It also allows for large purchases to be spread over several years and to be procured in installments.

Coupled with planning is the annual budgeting process. The RSIC budget is compiled from requirements generated by customers and staff. RSIC is multi-agency funded, and receives research and development dollars which provide for two years from obligation to disbursement. Overall budget ceilings are provided by each agency prior to the budgeting process. Requirements are received from customers and library staff, and prioritized against the budget ceilings with any requirements over budget ceilings provided as unfinanced requirements which may be provided if money becomes available. Dollars for the RSIC budget come directly from the customers through an overhead account.

RSIC is an Army operated multi-agency library. Organizationally, it is under the Army Research Development and Engineering Center (RDEC). The trend toward placing libraries under the corporate information office has not been used at RSIC. Experience has demonstrated that the library is more successful with funding and services if placed as closely to the customer as possible, and the corporate information office at Redstone is organizationally outside the research and development directorate. The library director reports directly to the Chief Center Support Office which is an administrative directorate with budget, editing and publishing, and supply functions. The library operates autonomously in a separate physical location from the next level supervision and receives administrative supervision only; no technical supervision is provided.

Within RSIC, functional areas outline the organization. The Office of the Director has an administrative staff including budget, personnel, and secretarial staff. The translations area also reports directly to the director. Branches include Reference and Technical Services with the systems office operating under Technical Services. Each branch is headed by a supervisor who reports to the director. No more than two levels of supervision exist in the organization. Communications among staff members occur through meetings, E-mail, informal conversations, and messages. Further information may be disseminated as needed. Employees submit key events brief forms through their supervisor to the director on a daily basis, pointing out key events in their areas. Meetings with all staff are held as needed. Time is blocked out on Mondays from 8 to 11 a.m. for the purpose of holding meetings, establishing dialogue, or providing training as needed.

SERVICES

Services to the customers include providing a "one-stop" shop for scientific and technical information, access to the library and other libraries' resources through remote and on-site access to their databases, specific answers to technical questions by reference staff, providing library staff on research and development teams working on special projects, assistance with the activity's technology transfer program, courier service to deliver the information to the customer, and technical assistance on information technology problems and issues.

Special services include the operation of contractor reading rooms, the imaging and archiving of project office documents, and the creation of CD-ROM products for the customer. At the heart of all services is the in-house computer. In 1967 RSIC developed one of the first in-house computers which computerized various library functions such as cataloging, acquisitions, and serials (Hayes, 1967). That system evolved through the years and was replaced in 1990 by the acquisition of a commercially available UNIX-based integrated library system called STILAS (Scientific and Technical Information Library Automation System). Developed for the scientific and technical community from a prototype designed at the Defense Technical Information Center (DTIC), the STILAS system provides for computerization of all library functions. Remote access is available through two separate networks for RSIC Army and NASA customers. Two computers for open and closed literature operate to manage and make accessible the library's collection. As with any information technology product, the system is constantly evolving and incorporating changes as technology changes.

STAFF

The staff consists of 32 government employees who are librarians, technical information specialists, library technicians, and translators, and 15 contract personnel working under a library support contract. The library staff is a stable workforce with an average of 15 years' service at RSIC. Because of the complexity of the collection and the information required, librarians usually work three to five years before becoming experts with the collection. As one customer put it, "The RSIC reference librarian has the equivalent of a PhD in several disciplines gained through experience with interfacing with the customer." The staff's emphasis on service is reflected by the heavy usage by customers and positive feedback on customer surveys (Botta, 1991).

Translations are provided from Russian, German, French, Spanish, and Japanese into English and are performed by in-house staff and under contract. Some machine translation is utilized for efficiency and timeliness of delivery.

RSIC has cooperative education contract with an accredited library school, and recruits graduate cooperative education students who balance work and school and are given work assignments in all functional areas of the library. Upon successful completion of the assignment, they can be non-competitively converted to librarian positions if there are vacancies. RSIC also is the training site for interns hired into the Army Materiel Command Librarian Intern Program. These are candidates with library degrees who are selected for a one-year training program at RSIC and are then offered positions within the command where vacancies exist.

Keeping a trained staff technically up-to-date is critical for the success of the organization. Courses in database searching, information technology, and other library-related subjects are brought to the work site, and staff is trained on site. Staff also attend professional conferences and serve on various committees of professional organizations where information is exchanged. Teleconferences are used as effective tools to keep staff informed. Interactive television has been used successfully with the University of Alabama School of Library and Information Studies to teach courses that allow the staff to attend on the work site. Library technicians are enrolled in undergraduate courses both during and after duty hours. Upon completion, they are provided opportunities for graduate library science courses as part of their individual development plans. Tuition assistance and work time are provided for attendance at these classes. Librarians on the staff compete with other librarians for developmental assignments. These include management and leadership assignments, networking assignments, and short computer courses.

Each summer RSIC participates in the Army's High School Math/Science Faculty Program. This program brings high school math and science teachers into the research and development environment where they work under ten-week contracts performing research projects. This program has been utilized by RSIC since 1989 to provide five to six research projects on scientific and technical information; the teachers perform the research, write a technical report of their findings, and their information is used to help understand RSIC customers and to be able to predict trends in the utilization of RSIC. The teachers acquire additional skills from performing the research that enhance their teaching abilities when they return to the classroom.

MARKETING

Success in providing scientific and technical information services requires constant marketing of these services. Each library staff member is a public relations person for the organization. A marketing plan has been developed that has proved effective in disseminating information to the customer. This plan includes marketing materials such as brochures, E-mail, orientations, videos, newspaper articles, electronic bulletin boards, and utilization of listservs available on Internet. Successful marketing requires that you go where the customer gets information. Externally, RSIC has information on its services imbedded into customer information channels such as organization newsletters and electronic mail. Other mechanisms have been used, evaluated, and discontinued if not effective. Effective marketing requires identification and follow-up to determine effectiveness.

The bottom line is that no matter how good the marketing plan, if the scientist or engineer customer does not perceive that information or services are easily accessible and relevant, they will not be used.

EVALUATION

Like marketing, evaluation is a constant activity in any service organization. RSIC distributes surveys to its customers every two years to determine effectiveness and to validate its planning strategy. An electronic suggestion file is available for suggestions.

Seven criteria for performance evaluation have been identified and have been tracked for five years. This data has been utilized to establish new services, to change existing services, and to defend budget requirements. Benchmarking services with other organizations have also been effective in evaluating service quality. The best evaluation comes from the customer. Bringing the customer into internal meetings has been an effective way to get feedback on services. Customers also give testimonials on services performed in reference areas. The key element to success in evaluation is follow-up with feedback to the customer. This is completed through formal correspondence, E-mail, and verbal conversation. It is an ongoing process that is never completed.

In today's environment providing scientific and technical information is both exciting and challenging. The rapid changes underway are providing opportunities for excellence and barriers to overcome. As super computer highways become realities, RSIC will be positioned with its collection, its dedicated staff, and its entrepreneurial and innovative spirit to be an important contributor on the electronic network.

REFERENCES

Botta, Sandra. 1991. *Results of Redstone Scientific Information Center 1991 Survey.* Redstone Arsenal, AL: August.

Hayes International Corporation. 1967. *Automated Literature Processing Handling and Analysis System.* First Generation. Redstone Arsenal, AL: U.S. Army Missile Command, June.

Long, Randy Lee. 1993. *Interlibrary Loan Survey.* Redstone Arsenal, AL: 24 August.

Orne, Jerrold; Shipman, Joseph; and Vosper, Robert. 1961. *Report of a Survey of Library Facilities and Services at Redstone Arsenal.* Redstone Arsenal, AL: June.

Redstone Scientific Information Center. 1988. *A Five Year Plan: Redstone Scientific Information Center (fiscal years 1989-1993).* Redstone Arsenal, AL: April.

STATISTICAL INFORMATION

Sponsor: U.S. Army Missile Command and Marshall Space Flight Center

Name of Unit: Redstone Scientific Information Center

Location: Building 4484
Redstone Arsenal, Alabama
35898-5241

Name of Head of Unit: Sybil H. Bullock

Title of Head of Unit: Director

Title of Immediate Supervisor: Director, Center Support Office

Staff Size: 20 professionals; 27 non-professionals

Main Subjects Collected: Missile and Space Technology, Aeronautics, Navigation, Guidance and Control, Space Defense, Propulsion, Chemistry, Directed Energy, Computer Science

Collection Size:

Books:	284,000
Current subscriptions:	5,427
Bound journal volumes:	100,115

Pamphlets: 5,000
Reports: 1,300,000 unclassified
700,000 classified

Special Collections: German World War II Archives, Peenemunde Papers, Metrication Collection, Rocketry Historical Collection, Patents, AIAA Papers, Specifications and Standards

Computer Services: DIALOG, STN, BRS, DROLS, DMS, DILSIE, NASA RECON, LEXIS, NEXIS, OCLC, WUIS, IR&D, Periscope

Number of Users: 111,000
(FY1993)

Area of Unit: 100,000 sq. ft.

Number of Seats for Users: 150

PART IV:
INDEPENDENT AGENCIES

Chapter 6

Research Library of the Board of Governors of the Federal Reserve System

Ann Roane Clary

INTRODUCTION AND DESCRIPTION

The Board of Governors of the Federal Reserve System, in Washington, DC, occupies two main buildings located between Constitution and Virginia Avenues, NW. These buildings are surrounded by the Department of State, the National Academy of Sciences, the Interior Department's Bureau of Indian Affairs, and the Vietnam Memorial. The Lincoln Memorial is within a few blocks, and from the roof level terrace of the Board's Martin building there is a panoramic view of the Washington Monument, the Jefferson Memorial, and Arlington House, the home of Robert E. Lee.

The Research Library, the subject of this chapter, is located in the older of the two office buildings (see Photo 6.1). It was dedicated by President Franklin D. Roosevelt on October 20, 1937, and was later named for one of the Board's prominent chairmen, Marriner S. Eccles. The more modern Federal Reserve building, built just across the street during the early 1970s, was designated the William McChesney Martin, Jr. building in honor of another outstanding chairman. (Although the staff typically refers to the locations as the Board and Martin buildings, the press occasionally cites the former edifice, which houses the Board member's offices, as the "marble palace.")

The Federal Reserve System dates back to 1913 when the Federal Reserve Act was signed into law on December 23 by President Woodrow Wilson, thereby reestablishing what eventually became a

Photo 6.1. Research Library of the Board of Governors of the Federal Reserve System. Courtesy of Board of Governors of the Federal Reserve System.

central bank and a successor to the First and Second Banks of the United States.

The Board of Governors of the Federal Reserve System, best described as an independent agency within the framework of the government, is responsible for formulating and conducting monetary policy with supervisory and regulatory responsibility over those banks that are members of the Federal Reserve System. (All national banks which are chartered by the Comptroller of the Currency are required to become members of the System, and commercial banks, chartered by their states, may be members if they can qualify.) Also included within the System are 12 Federal Reserve Banks with 25 branches.

The seven board members are appointed by the President of the United States and must be confirmed by the United States Senate. Their terms of office are staggered, with a full term lasting for 14 years. A chairman and vice chairman are appointed by the President for four-year terms, and both of these terms are renewable. (Over time, the Federal Reserve Chairman has been referred to as the second most influential American, next only to the President.)

In order to operate the country's central bank, the Board of Governors has approximately 1,600 staff members working in 15 divisions in a variety of positions including economists, attorneys, statisticians, accountants, librarians, computer experts, editors, and numerous other support groups. Many of the staff hold doctoral degrees and/or are highly educated in their selected fields. The employees, other agencies' personnel, and the public have access to two libraries within the Board: the Research Library, which is part of the Division of Research and Statistics, and the Law Library, whose librarian reports to the Legal Division. While the focus of this discussion is management within the Research Library, it would be remiss not to stress the importance of the Law Library to both the Board and its users from the outside.

Volumes from a National Monetary Commission collection, which were originally housed at the Library of Congress, were sent on permanent loan to the Federal Reserve Board in 1914 or 1915, and these were the nucleus around which a Board collection evolved. In fact, an annual report indicated that a collection, of sorts, was begun as early as 1914.

The Board's first librarian was not appointed until 1918, and since the library was established, there have been only seven chief librarians overseeing its operation. Currently the library has a staff of 11: six librarians and five library technicians. Many of the staff members have worked at the Board for a substantial number of years and, therefore, are thoroughly familiar with the library's functions as well as with the Board's structure and type of research needs.

The main subject matter in the library collection includes monetary and fiscal policy; banking, both domestic and foreign; finance; mathematics; economics; and economic conditions in the United States and abroad. There is a major special collection pertaining to the history and operation of the Federal Reserve System and another one on central banking. This consists mainly of annual reports and bulletins received under exchange agreements with central banks around the world. (Recognizing the importance of these collections has led the librarians in the past few years to focus on the preservation of this material as well as on the area of disaster planning.)

During my 31 years spent in the Research Library, 24 of which were as the chief librarian, I undoubtedly had the privilege of witnessing more extensive changes within the library field and the Research Library than my predecessors. Throughout most of those years, the present assistant chief librarian and I worked closely on numerous endeavors, with others on the staff contributing, concerning their particular areas of knowledge.

The late 1960s saw the establishment of a Committee on Library Functions, composed of the librarians from the Federal Reserve Banks and the Board; in the 1970s, the Research Library became a rotating member of the then Federal Library Committee, and in 1978 the library was designated as a Government Depository Library. During this period, we met with architects and members of a renovation committee to plan a new and more spacious library, which was completed in 1978. The placing of periodical subscriptions was turned over to a subscription agent during 1980; in 1981, the library joined the OCLC assisted cataloging system, and the staff began utilizing online reference databases as well.

In November 1984, a turnkey system from Innovative Interfaces was acquired in order to automate, in stages, the periodical, acquisitions, cataloging, and circulation records. (The system also allowed the library staff to track the status of the books and subscriptions budget on a daily basis instead of waiting for a monthly printout.) In the late 1980s, personal computers were procured to perform online searching, do word processing, search the online public access catalog (PAC), and to connect to OCLC and the mainframe computer. Finally, the library's system was linked to the Research Division's network in order to provide staff of the Board the capability of searching the PAC from their offices.

During 1989 and 1990, the library staff worked through a network on a retrospective conversion of the card catalog's pre-1981 records. Although the acquisition of CD-ROM technology was under consideration for several years, it did not become a reality until 1993, under my successor.

Providing enhancements to, or changes in, the library's methods of operation required many hours of planning and work by the librarians and technicians. I believe, however, that in retrospect, those who participated in implementing the automated systems would agree that the results were well worth the effort.

In the following pages, I shall address the various overall aspects of managing the Research Library, including the three units into which the library is divided: reader services, technical processing, and periodicals, each of which is supervised by a librarian. This internal division of functions is not without work flow flaws; but circumstances, including the configuration of the library's layout, have made it an acceptable one for the present time.

ORGANIZATION AND STAFFING

In order to provide better insight into the library's operation, a brief description of its areas and personnel follows (see Figure 6.1). General administration is, of course, provided by the chief librarian who is responsible for planning, staffing, and budgeting for the library's requirements, and representing the library at various meetings and conferences. The librarian reports to a division officer who, in turn, reports to the director of the Division of Research and Statistics.

Reader services is the province of the assistant chief librarian, and covers reference, book selection, acquisitions, and circulation, includ-

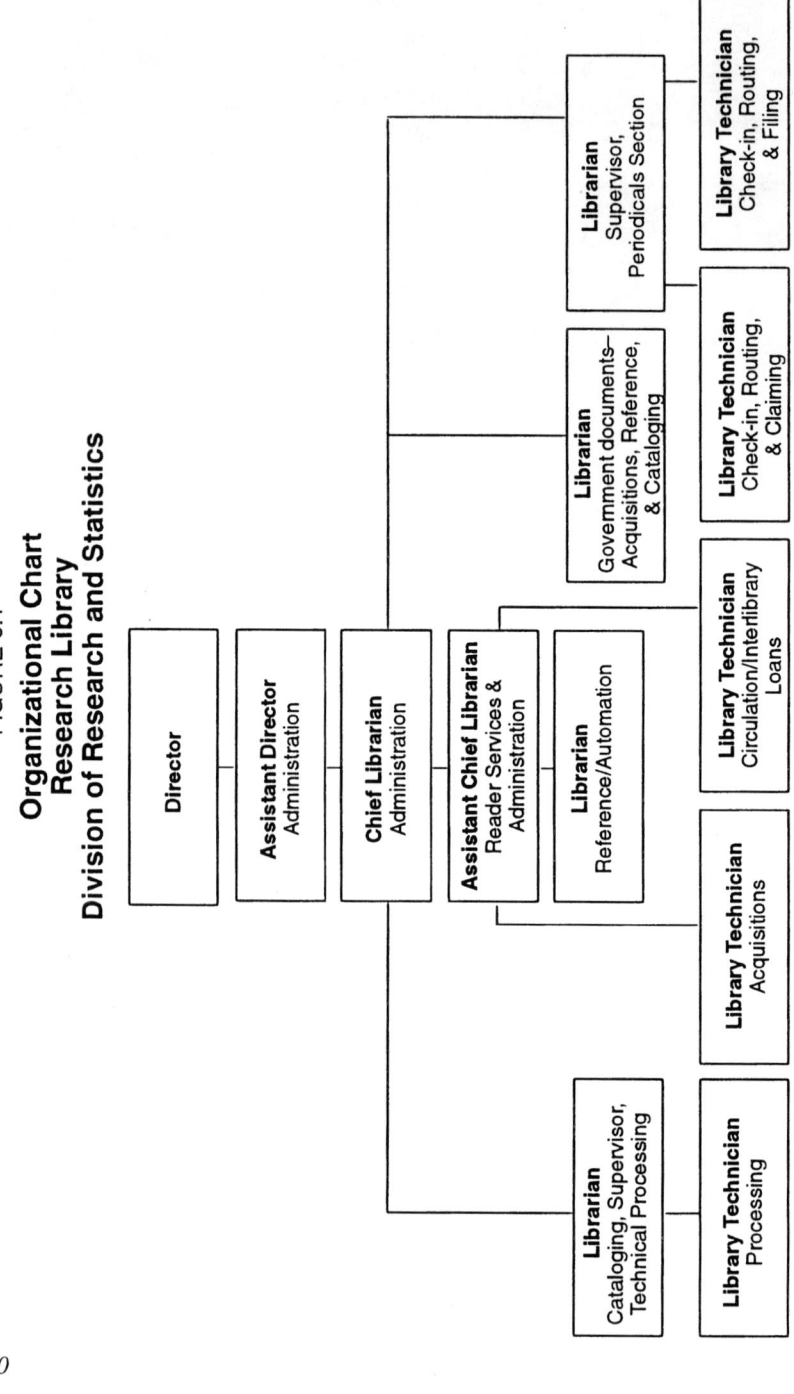

FIGURE 6.1
Organizational Chart
Research Library
Division of Research and Statistics

ing the interlibrary loan function. The staff includes a reference librarian, who not only assists with the reference work, including a phase of book selection, but also acts as the automation manager for the library. A third reference librarian is responsible for the acquisition and distribution of U.S. Government and international publications, combined with providing reference service on this body of literature and cataloging the congressional publications which she procures. This is an example of how staff members in a relatively small library must be flexible and assume the responsibility for several library activities.

Support staff within reader services includes two library technicians, one who handles acquisitions and tracks the books and subscriptions expenditures, and a second, who is responsible for the circulation of books and bound periodicals, collection maintenance, and the interlibrary loan function.

As a person leaves reader services, located in the front part of the library, and starts down a corridor toward the periodical section, a stop along the way affords access to the technical processing office with a staff of two employees: the cataloger librarian, who is head of this area, and a library technician who assists her. With a small staff to handle cataloging and related book processing, the addition of the OCLC capability, more than a decade ago, was anticipated as a means of keeping the cataloging of material more current.

The cataloger is expected to stay abreast of enhancements to this system, and other related technology, in order to make software and equipment recommendations to the chief librarian and keep this unit functioning at the highest possible level. In addition, the library technician is responsible for acquiring a sizable number of annual volumes received on a gratis or exchange basis. Both the technician and the librarian participate in phases of preparing and receiving the publications which are sent out to a bindery.

From the technical processing area it is only a few steps to the periodical section, which is headed by a librarian who supervises two library technicians. This librarian oversees the organization, routing, and maintenance of the periodical collection, which contains many foreign as well as domestic titles. She must also deal with the Board's staff concerning their needs and/or problems relating to this body of literature and its availability.

The library technicians handle the receipt, routing, claiming, and shelving/filing of periodicals and work with the librarian on the preparation of journals forwarded to the bindery. The ability to check-in, claim, and route material via the INNOPAC (Innovative Interfaces Online Public Access Catalog) system has resulted in a more efficient operation, both here and throughout the library.

Before concluding this discussion, one additional staffing resource should be mentioned: the student aide. As the library staff has typically had difficulty in finding sufficient time to promptly cope with many of the more routine tasks, the resulting backlogs have, on occasion, been a cause for concern. During more recent years, the Division of Human Resources Management has been able to supply the library with a part-time high school or college student aide, which has been a major source of assistance, especially when the person is detail-oriented, flexible, and receptive to a library environment. (The aide may be assigned to any area, but is most likely to work in the periodical section and/or reader services.)

COLLECTION DEVELOPMENT

The continuous building of a collection to meet the Board's growing and ever changing needs is one of the most important functions of the library, and it takes place mainly within the reader services area. Books and journals acquired through interlibrary loans can satisfy short-term requirements, but the library staff should be kept informed of new initiatives and assignments that will necessitate the purchase of specialized material.

Over the years, the collection has been built through purchases, donations, and the exchange of publications with other institutions, in addition to material acquired as a Government Depository Library. As noted previously, the assistant chief librarian is responsible for book selection, reviewing selection tools, publishers' catalogs, and acquisition lists from other libraries for publications of interest. The chief librarian approves most of the items recommended for purchase, rejects some, and earmarks others for future acquisition when funds become available.

There are many Board initiatives that require special purchasing. The library buys some of these publications, while others that are intended for use exclusively within one area may be paid for by the division requesting the material. This procedure developed because there are usually more items proposed for purchase than the library's budget can accommodate.

A Friends of the Library group, established within the past few years, has been assisting in collection development by recommending the acquisition of books in their fields of expertise, such as automation, economic theory, and mathematics. Previously, the library had sent out annual budget calls to the divisions, requesting a list of their book and subscription needs, but it was decided that, in some instances, insufficient time or thought went into these proposals and that another approach would be preferable. The library now encourages that requests be made throughout the year, as long as they are approved by their division-designated staff member.

A major problem continues to be the number of periodical subscriptions that the library is asked to buy. Some suggestions are for journals that are being newly introduced, while others are for a second or third copy of a periodical that is currently being received. It is now stipulated that a new journal may be ordered only after it has been reviewed by the requesting area and not just selected from reading an advertisement. An effort is also made to cancel titles that are no longer as useful as they once were. Therefore, a new copy must undergo close scrutiny prior to ordering.

In addition to the Board's staff, scholars, college and university students, and the general public utilize the Research Library's collection. The library is open to visitors one day a week, but upon special request exceptions may be made. Visitors can consume a large portion of the staff's time, thereby delaying their work on behalf of the Board's staff. On the other hand, however, it is important to share resources as much as possible since some of the material is unique to the Research Library.

PLANNING AND BUDGETING

The organization and staffing of a library, as well as the acquisition and maintenance of a collection, dictate that every effort be made to plan and budget judiciously. In the Division of Research and Statistics, these functions are done in tandem. Section chiefs prepare budget-planning documents, which are submitted to the division every spring and then reviewed during a meeting with the division officers. At that time, questions are posed, and proposals are explained or defended. As a result some proposals may be modified, postponed, or withdrawn, while others are approved, and perhaps even expanded.

The program budget outlines accomplishments over the past year and lists projects planned for the coming year, including the names of the participating staff members and a designation as to the importance of the undertaking: high, medium, or low priority.

The library's overall objectives are included in the report as, for example, the objectives in 1986 to 1987 were: (1) to provide the Board's staff, on a timely basis, with continued high quality reference service as well as current research material; (2) to prepare for further automation of library functions and, having evaluated the INNOVACQ (now INNOPAC) online public access catalog and circulation modules, make recommendations based upon our criteria versus INNOVACQ's capabilities; (3) to continue, through such channels as library publications, Board-wide notices, meetings, and library tours, to inform the Board's staff of the wealth of library resources and services that can enrich their research activities.

Another section lists ongoing activities, as for example producing library publications, and such routine procedures as the continuous review of periodical subscriptions to evaluate their current value and/or possible cancellation. Returning to the 1986/87 budget program, it concluded with a section covering the library's projected needs, plans, and concerns for the period from 1988 to 1991. One of the concerns related again to periodical literature and how to maintain an outstanding library collection with continuing price increases, in particular, for journal subscriptions. An ongoing goal had been to have an integrated system installed by 1990 and, fortunately, the library staff was able to achieve this goal.

In conjunction with the budget program document, the following additional information, with justification, is usually provided to the division: staffing requirements; requests for automation funding; the need for new furniture, equipment, and supplies; a recommendation for any facet of the work that should be contracted out; a proposal for the services of a consultant; an estimation of the funding required for outside conferences, seminars, and workshops; a projected amount for the binding budget; and a list of library publications planned for the coming year.

When the chief librarian meets with the division officers, at length during the spring planning session and, briefly, the following January, the major budget program topics are discussed. These include library staffing, any problems concerning meeting the current year's objectives, and significant upcoming initiatives.

During August or September, the library forwards its books and subscriptions budget to the division. The line officer has already relayed guidelines for the targeted percentage increase for the next year, and unless the budget total substantially exceeds this amount, it has a reasonable chance of being approved. For the library's benefit only, the budget is divided into categories such as books, periodicals, government documents, etc., in order to provide better monitoring and dissuade over expending in some areas to the detriment of others. As mentioned previously, implementation of the INNOPAC system enabled the staff to track expenditures online, on a daily basis.

Between April and September, an extensive amount of planning and budgeting is done at the section level. There is also planning within the library which involves all of the staff at one time or another. The major portion of this activity logically falls to the chief and assistant chief librarians, but some phase of planning is usually on the agenda for the monthly meeting of the library staff. This meeting also provides a forum for updates on library initiatives, accomplishments, and special announcements. In addition, each staff member is encouraged to inform the group regarding important activities within his or her unit.

Out of the above sessions evolve meetings of the six librarians, held as needed. An agenda is prepared by the chief librarian and usually focuses on current projects or problems. These group discussions are frequently both lively and productive in the areas of communicating and decision making.

Some years ago we discovered during our selection of an automated system that it was most important to involve not just the librarians in the process but, as much as possible, the entire staff. This was a positive experience that resulted in a system which has served the library well and provides an interesting and challenging project for the participants.

MANAGEMENT AND TRAINING

In the preceding discussions, the chain of command within the division and in the library has been outlined. This section emphasizes an effective management tool and staff training opportunities.

The chief librarian reports to the assistant director in charge of administration in the Division of Research and Statistics. His or her approval is required on major library policy decisions as well as personnel actions and automation proposals. When in doubt, the librarian informs the assistant director of contemplated initiatives in order to have backing and/or assessment of their merit and their chance of division acceptance.

The division director, with the official staff present, holds monthly meetings with the section chiefs, of whom the librarian is one. Section chiefs in turn, notify the division of the date and time of their section meetings in the event that an officer wishes to be present. Therefore, the level of communication within the division and section can be rated as within an acceptable range.

Section chiefs are expected to select from and attend management sessions held by the training staff from the Division of Human Resources Management. Some of the recent topics included:

Basics of Supervision	Effective Oral Communications
Defining Leadership	Managing Time Productively
Interviewing and Selection	Setting Performance Expectations and Providing Performance Feedback
Skills for Managers	EEO/Legal Considerations in the Interview and Selection Process

Special courses and lectures are also offered for the secretarial and support staff. Employees are eligible to attend training sessions in such areas as:

Adapting to Change	Discover the Purposes and Functions of the Federal Reserve Board Series (Noontime lecture)
Performance Management Program	
Stress Management	

The number and variety of training opportunities has increased significantly in recent years, with computer-oriented sessions also available to the staff.

One of the training courses listed above focuses on the Performance Management Program, better known as PMP. This program is an annual review of each employee's job performance. For many years, the reviews for the library technicians and assistants were conducted by their immediate supervisors. More recently, however, following changes in the nature and format of the reviews, the chief librarian has held the reviews after conferring with the line officer to discuss staff achievements and/or potential problems. This approach should result in more uniform ratings, which is of particular importance since the performance rating now more closely affects the salary increases than in the past. Unless the rating is unsatisfactory, each employee receives a percentage increase in salary during the next year based on such factors as the strength of the PMP rating, the employee's placement within a matrix, salary alignment with other staff, recent salary history, and funds available in the division's merit budget.

A brochure distributed by the Division of Human Resources Management listed for employees the following components of their PMP reviews:

Defining your job responsibilities
Identifying your specific performance objectives and how your performance will be evaluated
Providing periodic reviews to help you keep on track or to change your performance objectives, if necessary
Providing an annual overall performance review
Identifying development needs to improve your work performance and further your career at the Board

The chief librarian holds staff PMPs between August 1 and October 31, with the employees receiving one of the following ratings: (1) Outstanding, (2) Commendable, (3) Satisfactory, or (4) Unsatisfactory. If the employee believes that the evaluation is unfair, it may be appealed.

The performance review is an important management tool when it is used in conjunction with the chief librarian's general monitoring of the library's operation throughout the year. A significant portion of the librarian's time is spent in evaluating each staff member and assigning a rating so that the individual is rewarded fairly with any salary increase that is merited. It also requires the employee's efforts to demonstrate any progress over the last 12 months. Some evaluations can result in less than enthusiastic receptions by employees; however, the PMP benefits the person who meets or excels in his or her job performance, and it should also open up a dialog with those who could improve their ratings.

ADMINISTRATIVE SUPPORT

Generally, over the period that I served as the chief librarian, I was pleased with the administrative support that the library received from a total of eight line officers. Each of them listened as I brought my proposals and problems to him or her and offered me solutions and/or alternatives as they saw them.

I found two impediments, however, during these years. Most of the officers had numerous responsibilities in their own fields of expertise and also had other sections for which they acted as line officers. Through no fault of their own, their time for any one area was limited. More importantly, however, was the fact that the majority of those with whom I dealt were economists who used the library and/or had material routed to them but did not completely understand the library world with its unique problems and its own language. Granted, it is difficult for any one who has never been employed in a library to comprehend the full impact of some library problems or the need for new services or equipment with which he is unfamiliar. Routine jobs are not always uncomplicated and what appears on the surface to be a simple task can consume an untold number of hours.

There is no "quick" solution to these difficulties other than to continue to "market" the library at every opportunity and use the budget program meetings with the division officers to stress the importance of a well staffed and equipped library to a research-oriented institution.

FACILITIES AND EQUIPMENT

Since 1978, when the library moved into a renovated location within the Board building, it has been able to provide adequate space and equipment for its users as well as an attractive library complete with marble accents and works of art. (For a year or two, the library had a Georgia O'Keeffe painting on loan and, more recently, it has acquired a permanent collection of framed photographs pertaining to the history of the Federal Reserve System.)

There are two reading rooms located in the front part of the library. The one on the entrance level contains the general reference collection and has space for eight readers. On the lower level, which can be reached by an internal elevator, a large circular table easily accommodates six people and provides a pleasant location for conducting research or holding a meeting. A skylight above the table gives a sense of openness and also encourages the growth of plants banked against one wall. The shelves are filled with sets of banking, business, and finance volumes. Both of the levels also have room for those who prefer to work at study carrels, as does the periodical section.

The reader services area is just inside of the library's front door and, as one enters, directional signs clearly indicate the information and circulation desks. Instructional signs are also posted by the PAC terminals and the "frozen" card catalog which contains references to some unique material which may never be included in the online catalog. There is a shelf of recent acquisitions readily available for browsing, and nearby is the chief librarian's office, which was placed here in order to make the librarian readily accessible to both library users and the staff.

Close to the reference desks is the terminal where the librarians search the various databases to supply requested information for library users. Employees have access to the online catalog from both the library and Board offices. The library staff members have PCs and/or terminals on their desks; the OCLC database is at hand for those members who need to utilize it frequently; and printers are located throughout the library. A microfilm/fiche reader-printer is available in a small room, complete with storage cabinets, and a second fiche reader is found in the bookstacks area. A photocopier is situated in the periodical section, and a FAX machine is only a short distance across the hall from the library in a telecommunications center.

The library offers a quiet, pleasant environment conducive to research and to productivity as well. The majority of the staff have a window within sight of their desks and, as the library overlooks a courtyard, there is a feeling of serenity within a bustling city. From the windows one can see a fountain, dogwood trees, crepe myrtle, and camellia bushes. (When the winters are mild, the camellias continue to bloom throughout the season.) Spring brings daffodils and rhododendron blossoms, in addition to the dogwood. During the summer, the courtyard is made available to the Board employees who can eat their lunches at umbrella tables that are interspersed with tubs of red or pink geraniums. This is an appropriate location for a facility such as a library, where staff and library users alike can share the view.

NETWORKING: TWO CONTEXTS

When the Research Library joined OCLC, it was through the FEDLINK network, a branch of the Federal Library and Information Center Committee located at the Library of Congress. Coming soon after OCLC was the acquisition of reference data bases: DIALOG, followed by the New York Times Information Bank which expanded the reader services area's ability to search a much broader field of literature in a brief period of time. NEXIS and the Dow Jones News Retrieval Services were added later. The most recent library innovation is the ability to access the telecommunications network, the Internet.

The addition of CD-ROM is providing another dimension of resources to library users. Econlit searching is available, covering information in the *Journal of Economic Literature*. Also procured was the Joint Bank-Fund (World Bank and International Monetary Fund) Library's bibliography of periodicals and research papers known as *IntlEc CD-ROM: The Index to International Economics, Development and Finance*. In addition, the library is utilizing WILSONDISC, which provides indexing and abstracting for 350 of the most popular business periodicals. Today, the possibilities for the rapid retrieval of information are growing steadily.

The perception of networking in the Research Library is that its benefits are twofold. First, through the electronic means of searching databases, the library is providing expanded reference service to the library user. This, in turn, improves the visibility of the library and designates it as a section that is in the forefront of automation.

To a research-oriented institution, this is invaluable, and each new initiative along this line continues to enhance the library's image.

The library has also benefited from networking in another sense—with other libraries and librarians. There are numerous libraries in the area with which it works closely, particularly in the interlibrary loan field, where there is daily cooperation. The closest that it comes to true networking in this context, however, is with the 12 Federal Reserve Bank Libraries, which are located throughout the country from Boston to Dallas, and Chicago to San Francisco. The libraries borrow books and periodicals from one another, seek assistance with reference questions, and exchange ideas and information as the need arises. The Research Library acquires selected government documents for the bank libraries in order to expedite their receipt of the documents, in particular such working tools as the *Economic Report of the President* and the budget documents. In turn, the bank libraries can identify items published within their districts and supply the Board with material or information as requested.

Back in the 1960s, the librarians, who had met informally at the annual Special Libraries Association conferences, were appointed as members of a newly established Committee on Library Functions under a System Research Advisory Committee. The committee continues today, with the main meeting being held in the fall at one of the Federal Reserve Banks and every other year at the Board of Governors. The agenda is filled with committee business and invited speakers who come from the Federal Reserve System or from the library/information field. Several years ago, when the committee met at the Federal Reserve Bank of Chicago, we were fortunate to have the Bank of England's librarian as a participant.

Areas of common interest are discussed in the committee meetings, and whenever cooperative efforts will benefit the members the matter is investigated. For example, several of the libraries using the same periodical vender, contracted for their service as an entity rather than separately or through a network. This move cut through the red tape and is proving to be mutually beneficial to the libraries and to the vendor. In another instance, all of the libraries joined in maintaining a union list of serials which was initiated by the Federal Reserve Bank of Atlanta. A third example occurred when the Federal Reserve Bank of Philadelphia some years ago started publishing *The Fed in Print*, an index to bank and Board booklets, articles, and working papers, with each library contributing its own indexing. Through this publication, subject access is available to an important body of literature which can be invaluable to scholars and libraries researching the fields of monetary policy, banking and finance, economic theory, and related areas that the Federal Reserve System addresses.

MARKETING AND EVALUATING

Marketing the Research Library is accomplished mainly by attempting to furnish the Board's staff with the best service possible and provide a library environment conducive to research. This may draw an economist to a secluded table on the lower level of the library where research can be pursued without interruption. During the lunch period, a staff member might be seen in a study carrel working on a college class assignment, while at the table under the skylight another person may be leafing through a popular magazine from a recreational collection donated by employees. Seasonal or other pertinent displays on the wall outside of the library call attention to the entrance, while a bulletin board just inside exhibits jackets from newly acquired books. This is a frequent stop for library users as they come and go.

New Board employees are invited to a monthly library orientation session which focuses on services to the staff. As they tour the facility, they are informed about the rules and regulations and see a brief demonstration of searching techniques on PAC. They are also given a packet of material including a library brochure, a monthly book acquisitions list, and an in-house weekly publication highlighting the contents of journals available for borrowing.

National Library Week is always observed in some fashion such as conducting library tours for all staff members who want to keep abreast of the latest innovations–perhaps another phase of automation. At times, a guest speaker is invited to discuss a pertinent topic or review a new book, while some years, the library staff may decide that it is time to honor those members of the Board's staff who have recently published a book.

There are numerous other means of marketing the library such as contributing an article to the house organ and forwarding announcements to be published in an employees' newsletter. Undoubtedly, each staff selects its own most effective means of marketing their library.

Turning to the evaluating process, it should be noted that the Research Library is informally evaluated throughout the year as the division officers use the collection and the library's services. They remember when service is inadequate, or they discover that a needed periodical has not been received for several months. At times there are plausible reasons for a work-related deficiency by the library staff, while on other occasions there is no valid excuse for the problem. It is important for the librarian to urge the staff to inform him or her when something is "amiss" rather than having to learn it through an unhappy library user, or even worse, the line officer. Conversely, users also offer compliments for jobs well done, either in person or by a memo or letter, the latter most likely received from a visiting scholar. (Copies of these letters can be forwarded to the officer for his or her information and should also be shown to the staff involved, noting their laudatory performances.)

The most comprehensive and formal evaluations in recent years, however, are those that have been conducted by Operations Review teams composed of peers drawn from the Federal Reserve Banks. A team has reviewed the Research and Statistics Division three times since the early 1980s, and a Federal Reserve librarian was a member of each team. Background information is forwarded to the librarian in advance of his or her arrival in Washington. The librarian then spends the better part of a week in the library talking with staff members, observing them at work, asking questions, questioning library users, and finally, reporting the findings to the review team and to the division. The latter has an opportunity to respond to concerns that have been raised, and the review concludes with the issuing of a written report by the Operations Review team.

Although quite time consuming, especially for the reviewing librarian, the review process is for the most part beneficial to the library. The team librarian can recognize merit in some proposals that the library staff have put forward and support their implementation. He or she can also bring to the librarian's attention areas where improvements could be made. Later follow-up on the recommendations is intended to confirm that an effort was put forth to improve or correct these situations.

CONCLUSION

Managing a library is as much a challenge as it would be to manage any business. There are problems to resolve, decisions to make, a need to listen to the library staff as they express their concerns or problems, and the importance of talking with library users who want to ask a question, voice a complaint, or, hopefully, at times, praise an employee who has gone out of the way to be helpful. The majority of the staff perform well and take satisfaction in their work, going beyond what might be expected of them. (As the librarian, there is no greater pleasure than to present an award to an outstanding employee.) Some employees, of course, are average producers, and there are usually one or two who can improve their performance significantly and should be expected to do so.

As in all but the one-person library, teamwork plays an important part in keeping the library functioning at a high level. The staff must interact with one another on a give and take basis, communicating freely, and notifying other areas of the library concerning such matters as significant new publications that have been acquired, the arrival of new Board staff members and the impending departure of others, changes that will affect them, and any information that will benefit the operation in their section. This can be done effectively through a brief staff meeting, a telephone call, or a memorandum circulated throughout the library, the means depending upon the urgency of the matter at hand.

Over the years, the Research Library has been fortunate to have had some outstanding members on its staff, and it has not been unusual for them to have accumulated from 20 to 40-some years of Board and/or library service. While there will always be occasional user complaints concerning library performance–the tardy receipt of publications, delayed interlibrary loans, or a lost book not yet replaced–one takes immense satisfaction in a staff that generally does its best, resulting in a library reputation of which they can all be proud.

STATISTICAL INFORMATION

Sponsor: Board of Governors of the Federal Reserve System

Name of Unit: Research Library

Location: 20th St. and Constitution Ave., NW
Washington, DC 20551

Name of Head of Unit: Susan R. Vincent

Title of Head of Unit: Chief Librarian

Title of Immediate Supervisor: Assistant Director (Administration), Division of Research and Statistics

Staff Size: 6 professionals; 5 non-professionals

Main Subjects Collected: Banking, Finance, Economics, Monetary and Fiscal Policy, Mathematics

Collection Size:

Books:	54,000
Current subscriptions:	1,700
Bound journal volumes:	12,000
Clippings:	2,200

Special Collections: History and Operation of the Federal Reserve System; Central Banks Publications

Computer Services: DIALOG, NEXIS, Dow Jones News Retrieval, OCLC

Number of Users: 2,600, including 400 visitors
(FY1993)

Area of Unit: 13,475 sq. ft.

Number of Seats for Users: 35

PART V:
NATIONAL LIBRARIES

Chapter 7

National Library Service for the Blind and Physically Handicapped

Frank Kurt Cylke

AUTHORITY

In accordance with the authority provided in 2 U.S.C. (U.S. Code) 135(a), 135(b), and 135(c), the National Library Service for the Blind and Physically Handicapped, Library of Congress (NLS), is responsible for administering the national program to provide reading materials for the nation's blind and physically handicapped residents and U.S. citizens living abroad. These materials consist of books and magazines as well as music scores and texts produced in raised characters, as sound recordings, and in other suitable formats.

BACKGROUND

With the cooperation of authors and publishers who grant permission to use copyrighted works, NLS staff selects and produces full-length books and magazines in braille and on recorded disc and cassette. Books are distributed to a cooperating network of regional and subregional (local) libraries where they are circulated to eligible borrowers. Magazines are mailed directly from the manufacturer. Reading materials and playback machines are sent to borrowers and returned to libraries by postage-free mail. Established by an act of Congress in 1931 to serve blind adults, the program was expanded in 1952 to include blind children, in 1962 to provide music materials, and again in 1966 to include individuals with other physical impairments that prevent the reading of standard print.

The NLS program is funded annually by Congress. The fiscal year 1993 appropriation is $45,316,582. Regional and subregional libraries receive funding from state, local, and federal sources. Free matter postage for transport of appropriate library materials is provided through the U.S. Postal Service. The combined expenditure for the program approximates $110 million.

All residents of the United States or citizens unable to read or use standard printed materials as a result of temporary or permanent visual or physical limitations may receive service. A survey found that two million persons with some type of visual impairment are eligible and another million with physical conditions such as paralysis, missing arms or hands, lack of muscle coordination, or prolonged weakness may be eligible for the use of reading materials in recorded form.

Books are selected on the basis of their appeal to a wide range of interests. Bestsellers, classics, biographies, fiction, and how-to books are in great demand. Titles expected to be extremely popular are produced on flexible disc in several thousand copies and circulated to borrowers within several months of their publication in print form. A limited number of titles are produced in Spanish and other languages for readers whose primary language is not English. Registered borrowers learn of new books added to the collection through two bimonthly publications, *Braille Book Review* and *Talking Book Topics*. Through a union catalog available on microfiche, in computerized form, and on CD-ROM, every network library and user has access to the entire NLS book collection and to the resources of cooperating agencies.

Seventy-one magazines on disc and in braille were offered in 1993. Readers may request free subscriptions to *U.S. News and World Report*, *National Geographic*, *Consumer Reports*, *Good Housekeeping*, *Sports Illustrated*, *Jack and Jill*, *The Atlantic*, and many other popular magazines. Current issues are mailed to readers at the same time print issues appear, or shortly thereafter. Magazines are selected in response to demonstrated reader interest.

Playback equipment is loaned free for as long as recorded materials are being borrowed. Talking-book machines are designed to play disc recorded books and magazines at 8 rpm and 16 rpm; cassette machines are designed for cassettes recorded at 15/16 ips and the standard speed of 1-7/8 ips on 2 and 4 sides. Readers with significantly limited mobility may request a remote-control unit; hearing-impaired readers may be eligible for an auxiliary amplifier for use with headphones. A cassette machine with features designed primarily for elderly persons is available.

Persons interested in music materials may receive them directly from the NLS Music Section. The collection consists of scores in braille and large type; textbooks and books about music in braille and large print; and elementary instruction for voice, piano, organ, guitar, recorder, accordion, banjo, and harmonica in recorded form.

Correspondence courses leading to certification in braille transcribing, literary, music, mathematics, and braille proofreading are offered. A similar certificate in braille proficiency is also available. Voice auditions and informal training are given to volunteer tape narrators affiliated with local recording groups. A directory of volunteer groups that produce books for libraries and individuals is published frequently. Volunteers may call on NLS staff for their expertise in braille transcription and recording techniques.

Questions on various aspects of blindness and physical handicaps may be sent to NLS or to any network library. This service is available without charge to individuals, organizations, and libraries. Publications of interest to handicapped persons and service providers are free on request.

The consumer relations officer maintains regular contact with consumer groups and individual users of the program to identify and resolve service problems, to assure that users' needs are being met and to help identify service needs. Participating in surveys, evaluating new equipment, and serving on advisory committees are some of the ways in which consumers contribute to program development.

The research program is directed toward improving the quality of reading materials and related equipment, controlling program costs, and reducing the time required to deliver services to users. Current research activities include: (1) the study of the centralization of the storage and delivery of braille books and NLS audio playback equipment; (2) the development of high-speed embossers for braille printing; (3) the application of digital techniques to NLS recorded material; and (4) the use of the latest advances in computer technology to provide automated communications links among NLS, participating libraries, book and magazine producers, and distribution centers.

FUNCTIONS AND RESPONSIBILITIES

In brief, the National Library Service for the Blind and Physically Handicapped is responsible for the:

- selection, copyright clearance, and procurement of reading materials for blind and physically handicapped individuals;
- distribution of the materials and relevant bibliographic information either directly or through cooperating state and local network libraries;
- design, development, and procurement of sound reproduction equipment and its distribution either directly or through cooperating agencies;
- establishment of standards and assurance of quality products and services;
- training, guidance, and coordination of volunteers to augment national and local resources;
- administration of a nationwide interlibrary loan program, and of an international gift, exchange, and interlibrary program;
- preparation for catalogs and other publications in printed form and in other media for blind and physically handicapped readers to ensure full use of the national program;
- provision of a national reference and referral service on all aspects of blindness and physical handicaps;
- development, maintenance, and circulation of a national collection of musical scores and texts; and
- monitoring network libraries for effective use of NLS/BPH resources at each site and providing guidelines and procedures manuals.

In short, NLS/BPH maintains active liaison with blind and physically handicapped individuals throughout the country, with cooperating state and local network libraries, with nonprofit and other organizations interested or active in services to blind and physically handicapped persons, and with federal, state, and local agencies.

NLS has, in the federal context, "custody" of all reading materials specifically intended for blind and physically handicapped individuals, including books and magazines in raised characters, sound recordings, and other applicable forms.

OFFICE OF THE DIRECTOR

The Office of the Director is responsible for formulating policy, program planning, and directing all activities, including coordinating both the Materials Development Division and the Network Division. The office plans and implements all automation activities, including assisting with those involved in the network of cooperating state and local libraries and agencies. It coordinates information on research and development projects, evaluation programs, and surveys, and provides liaison with other government or quasi-official agencies, such as the United States Postal Service. It also provides administrative services related to operating the physical facility.

Director

The Director is responsible for administration, planning, policy formulation, and recommendations, as well as direction and coordination of the entire program. The Director:

- Plans and develops the national program in accordance with the intent of Congress, library policies, technological progress, and the readers' requirements. Advises the Librarian of Congress and other Library officers on matters pertaining to proposed legislation, related programs for the blind and physically handicapped, relations with other government agencies, and policy formation. Responds to Congressional inquiries and requests; testifies before Congressional committees on budget and program matters.
- Has primary responsibility for formulating the annual budget estimate of NLS/BPH and for the justification and presentation to Congressional committees.
- Serves as principal representative of the Library of Congress in its relations with other national and international organizations interested in work which aids blind and physically handicapped persons, maintaining contact with leaders and officials of such

organizations, and participating in conferences, conventions, and other such meetings. Conducts special studies and investigations, and makes recommendations for programs and cooperative undertakings, looking toward providing a more complete service to blind readers. Coordinates the sale and exchange of materials for blind and physically handicapped persons with organizations around the world.
- Has administrative responsibility for assuring that NLS/BPH procures materials and services at the lowest possible cost consistent with the quality and timeliness of delivery required to meet its needs. Serves as Contracting Officer for NLS book contracts and as contract advisor for all other contracts. Approves concepts, projects, bid packages, and award recommendations. Appoints and provides administrative direction to project monitors.
- Serves as the designated official responsible for the health and safety of NLS staff and for space planning, maintenance, and utilization of the recently renovated Taylor Street Annex, a separate facility distant from Capitol Hill.
- Directs the overall program.

MANAGEMENT

On assuming responsibility for the program in July 1973, the incumbent Director observed a need for a comprehensive review of management practices. His view was supported both by Library of Congress management personnel and by management-level staff personnel within NLS. Thus, in September 1973 he asked to participate in the Association of Research Libraries' "Management Review and Analysis Program (MRAP)." Once accepted into the program, he appointed co-chairpersons and instructed the staff to democratically select a study team to review management practices to the point of changing what needed to be changed and adding what needed to be added.

To ensure the greatest degree of objectivity, the initial study was based on data gathered from a variety of sources. Several questionnaires were designed to determine management, staff, and library network views of strengths and weaknesses and staff opinions about the organization. Interviews with Library of Congress administrators also helped staff understand more fully the environment in which they operate.

The study was done by and for all levels of staff. Over 95 percent were directly involved in a variety of ways: completing questionnaires, granting oral interviews, and participating on task forces or the study team itself. Study team and task force members reviewed existing files and pertinent documents such as internal and network memos, and Library of Congress regulations.

Early in the program the study team began collecting information and drafting the sections on history, environmental trends, and mission, objectives, and goals. About midway through the effort, task forces were formed to study the following areas of management practice: planning, policy, management information, budgeting, staff development, leadership and supervision, organization, personnel, and communication. The task forces were each composed of four to six members representing all levels of the staff, and chaired by a study team member. Each task force had a slightly different method for gathering data. After the current status of each area was defined, the task force attempted to analyze the situation and to suggest possible solutions to any symptoms or problems that were discovered.

Task force findings were discussed with the study team to ensure that objectivity was maintained, content was accurate, and reasoning was logical. The Director also made his comments on each report. Finally, ideas that evolved were assembled, and four dominant themes were identified: concern for staff, written guidelines and standards, information flow, and planning and implementation.

Twenty-five specific recommendations were made. All were accepted and implemented. A sophisticated, participatory management style emerged.

Based on long-range objectives, identified by the Director, and current year appropriations, each NLS section prepares specific performance goals for review and approval by NLS administrators.

Section heads and staff officers prepare monthly statistical reports which are submitted to the administration for management review. Personnel status reports are prepared and distributed quarterly. Quarterly meetings are scheduled to review progress on the goals. A biweekly meeting of division chiefs, assistant division chiefs, section heads, assistant section heads, and staff officers is held to encourage sharing of information, to discuss new policies, and to explain projects and activities requiring program-wide input–for example, budget compilation. Each major organizational office–Office of the Director, Materials Development Division, and Network Division– holds regular meetings to resolve problems of an intersectional nature within those offices and to review progress on approved schedules, etc. Section heads are encouraged to hold brief meetings with their staff on a regular basis to provide for appropriate upward and downward communication. Each year there are two full meetings of the staff scheduled. These offer overviews of selected program activity, progress reports, and discussions of topics identified by the staff.

Monthly reports are provided throughout the organization. These are statistical where appropriate and narrative where not. At the end of a 12-month period, division chief and section head performance ratings are based upon performance to the self-identified goals.

BUDGET

As noted, the management philosophy emphasizes direct involvement of the staff in setting forth and meeting specific goals. When preparing the annual budget, the director outlines major goals and objectives. Each section then sets its own goals and objectives within those guidelines, indicating how available resources and funds will be allocated. After much discussion and manipulation, the annual Management Plan is produced. This plan outlines goals and details, who is responsible for each task, when the task is scheduled to be completed, and how much money is needed. In addition, the current budget is fitted within an overall five-year plan.

Staff involvement does not stop at developing the budget and setting the goals, but continues yearlong through the reports and meetings previously noted. Regular discussions are held to ascertain whether staff members are on target with respect to their tasks and goals. Revisions are made as needed. Again, this style of management began with the MRAP assessment in 1973 and has worked ever since.

Examples of success are easily identified. Since 1974 the NLS budget has grown from just under $9.9 million to $45.3 million in fiscal 1993. Readership has increased more than 140 percent, from 318,300 in 1974 to 765,000 in 1992. Production of cassette books has increased more than 2,490 percent, with 65 titles produced in fiscal 1974 and 1,838 titles produced in fiscal 1992.

DIVISION/SECTION/OFFICE FUNCTIONS

When considering the application of the NLS management style it is useful to review overall division and section responsibilities (see Figure 7.1).

In the Office of the Director, the Administrative Section is responsible for coordinating personnel transactions and maintaining all official files, travel, training, and other records concerning personnel administration; planning and implementing communication services; coordinating fiscal and contractual activities; and coordinating the management, operation, and maintenance of the physical facility.

The Publications and Media Section is responsible for planning and implementing the publications, general information, exhibit, and other public education programs.

The Automation Office monitors development, implementation, and maintenance of customized computer programs for production control of books and magazines, circulation systems, inventory systems, bibliographic cataloging systems, and network communications systems.

It also:

- Coordinates installation and training for new computer systems.
- Analyzes software and hardware needs of staff, orders software and hardware, and provides training for use of software when appropriate.
- Advises managers as to possible uses of computers/software.
- Coordinates use of databases.
- Advises network libraries on automation activities.

The Research and Development Officer directs projects to research and develop new products or systems for use by patrons or network libraries.

118   MANAGEMENT OF FEDERALLY SPONSORED LIBRARIES

FIGURE 7.1. National Library Service overall division and section responsibilities.

**National Library Service
for the Blind and
Physically Handicapped**

Washington, DC 20542
Telephone (202) 707-5100
Fax (202) 707-0712
TWX 710-822-1969

The Library of Congress

Contact List

OFFICE OF THE DIRECTOR

Director, Frank Kurt Cylke
Assistant to the Director, Marvine R. Wanamaker
Program Management Assistant,
 Alice G. Freeman
Secretary, Sheryl A. Smith
Automation Officer, Robert J. McDermott
Assistant to the Automation Officer,
 Lloyd E. Lewis
Research and Development Officer,
 Michael M. Moodie
Postal Liaison, Thomas J. Martin

Administrative Section
Head, William Price
Assistant Head, Marsha Jackson
Contract Specialist, Lee Hurwitz

Publications and Media Section
Head, Robert E. Fistick
Assistant Head, Margaret Gresh Cytron
NLS News, Vicki Fitzpatrick

MATERIALS DEVELOPMENT DIVISION
Chief, Henry B. Paris, Jr.
Assistant Chief, Stephen E. James
*Equipment and Materials Maintenance
 Coordinator,* John R. Reiner
*Assistant Equipment and Materials Maintenance
 Coordinator,* Kevin M. Watson
Equipment Control Officer, James Miller

Bibliographic Control Section
Head, Robert Axtell

Braille Development Section
Head, Claudell Stocker
Assistant Head, Mary Lou Stark
Braille Instructor, Linda Bobo
Braille Music Advisor, Sandra Walberg Kelly
Braille Technology Advisor, John R. Jackson
Literary Braille Advisor, John E. Wilkinson

Collection Development Section
Head, Caroline Longmore
Assistant Head, Joan B. Bregger
Children's and Young Adult Librarian,
 Charlynn Spencer Pyne
Foreign Language Librarian, James R. Herndon
Copyright Permissions Assistant, Joyce A. Worthy

Engineering Section
Head, John P. Cookson
Audio Book Production Specialist, Billy R. West

Production Control Section
Head, Lois M. Mandelberg
Assistant Head, John Bryant
Studio Director, Harold R. Schneider

Quality Assurance Section
Head, Robert Kost
Assistant Head, Donald H. Smith

NETWORK DIVISION
Chief, Miriam M. Pace
Assistant Chief, Thomas J. Martin
Consumer Relations Officer, Judith M. Dixon

Inventory Management Section
Head, Leon Goode
Assistant Head, Janifer Burton
XESS Coordinator, Dorothy Moore

Music Section
Head, Shirley P. Emanuel

Network Services Section
Head, selection in process
Bibliographer, Catherine O'Connor
Network Consultants
 North/West, Stephen Prine
 South/Midlands, Devon S. Liner
 Services to U.S. Citizens Abroad,
  Y. Rathan Raj
 International Interlibrary Loan,
  Thomas J. Martin

Reference Section
Head, Linda C. Redmond (acting)
Assistant Head, Linda C. Redmond
CMLS Coordinator, Barbara Peterman
*Government Information and Volunteer
 Specialist,* Freddie L. Peaco

May 1992

This person also:

- Coordinates projects aimed at improving services to patrons or reducing costs of existing services.
- Advises on matters related to new products and services.
- Stays abreast of advances in technology related to production and distribution of braille and recorded books and magazines.

MATERIALS DEVELOPMENT DIVISION

The Materials Development Division is responsible for managing activities related to the selection, development, production, distribution, control, and repair of reading materials and related equipment; establishing and assuring standards of quality for the products; monitoring contracts with and providing guidance for the agencies, organizations, associations, publishers, and firms that participate in providing reading resources and equipment; directing the activities of book and equipment advisory committees; and supervising the six sections that make up the division.

The Materials Development Division Office recommends policy formulation and program planning for research, development, design, production, testing, evaluation, procurement, initial distribution, inventory control, and logistical support of all matter. This includes recorded books and magazines on disc, magnetic tape, audio cassette, braille books and magazines, playback equipment, and accessories.

The Bibliographic Control Section is responsible for bibliographic processing, maintenance, and control of reading materials included in the national collection; establishing national cataloging standards; coordinating union catalog activities for cooperating libraries and service organizations; managing production of the computer output microform catalog and related products; and participating in professional developments in bibliographic control.

The Braille Development Section is responsible for developing and implementing research projects relating to braille, serving as the Library of Congress authority on all braille codes and maintaining liaison with other national braille authorities, and developing all technical braille specifications and initiating programs for product improvement. In addition, this section takes responsibility for planning and preparing guides and teaching manuals based on the literary, mathematics, and music codes for use by local braille transcription instructors who prepare students for certification; conducting teacher training workshops in the field; and training, certifying, and advising volunteers and others nationwide who produce and process books in braille.

The Collection Development Section is responsible for acquiring print books; evaluating and selecting appropriate reading materials to be recorded, transcribed into braille, or produced in any other form; maintaining an established flow of selections to initiate the production cycle; requesting copyright clearances; preparing concise, descriptive annotations for all materials produced; maintaining liaison with publishers and authors; coordinating collection development program activities, advisory committees, and the foreign-language program; and identifying titles for replacement or withdrawal.

The Engineering Section is responsible for the design, development, specification, production release, and configuration control of all audio product accessories and processes; determining the method of measurement for all technical specifications; certifying compliance of the preproduction models with the specifications; maintaining awareness of state of the art developments applicable to audio technologies; and conducting continual programs for product improvement and innovation.

The Production Control Section is responsible for overseeing the production of books selected for the program, and executing database operation and administration of the Management Information and Production Information Systems used. Responsibilities include supervising and coordinating production and distribution of reading materials in recorded, braille, and other formats; scheduling and assigning materials for production to manufacturers and volunteer agencies; monitoring and controlling the status, cost, and distribution of reading materials and containers in production; financial analysis and forecasting of contracts by media; and providing detailed reports for use by all levels of management and contractors to direct, evaluate, and control production operations.

The Recording Studio unit of the Production Control Section is responsible for scheduling and recording 100 titles annually; recording special projects as assigned by the director; purchasing and providing audio master tapes for volunteer producing groups; determining narration requirements for titles to be recorded, and providing guidance in this area to manufacturers and volunteers; and evaluating and testing new technologies directly related to audio/voice recording.

The Quality Assurance Section is responsible for guaranteeing that the quality and performance of all braille and audio products and processes meet the standards and specifications of NLS/BPH. This includes ascertaining that all technical specifications can be verified by standard measurements as part of the production process, that all potential contractors for production of materials have adequate quality assurance capabilities, and that all contracts and specifications contain adequate provisions to guarantee that the products will meet the required standards; and producing periodic reports on the performance of contractors.

NETWORK DIVISION

The Network Division is responsible for managing activities related to establishing, developing, guiding, and monitoring a network of more than 150 cooperating state and local libraries and agencies (see Figure 7.2) which deliver only machines offering direct library service to blind and physically handicapped residents of the United States, its territories and possessions, and U.S. citizens living abroad. This division works in maintaining close and active liaison with schools, health care facilities, and other organizations interested or active in services to blind and physically handicapped persons, with library schools, and with appropriate state and local agencies; determining user eligibility for service; monitoring the multistate center contracts; and supervising the four sections and the staff officer that make up the division.

The Network Division Office monitors the national network of cooperating state and local agencies; and recommends initiation, consolidation, or dropping of network agencies (see Figure 7.3). It plans and formulates policies and procedures, sets goals and objectives both for the division and for the national network.

The Consumer Relations Officer is responsible for establishing and maintaining active liaison with individual users and consumer groups; conducting continuing user surveys; disseminating information about user inquiries to NLS/BPH and network libraries; providing information and reference assistance to readers; and conducting user

FIGURE 7.2

National Library Service
for the Blind and
Physically Handicapped

The Library of Congress

Network of Major Service Centers

Key:
★ Library of Congress
◉ Multistate Center East
   (serves states east of dotted line)
◆ Multistate Center West
   (serves states west of dotted line)
• Regional Libraries

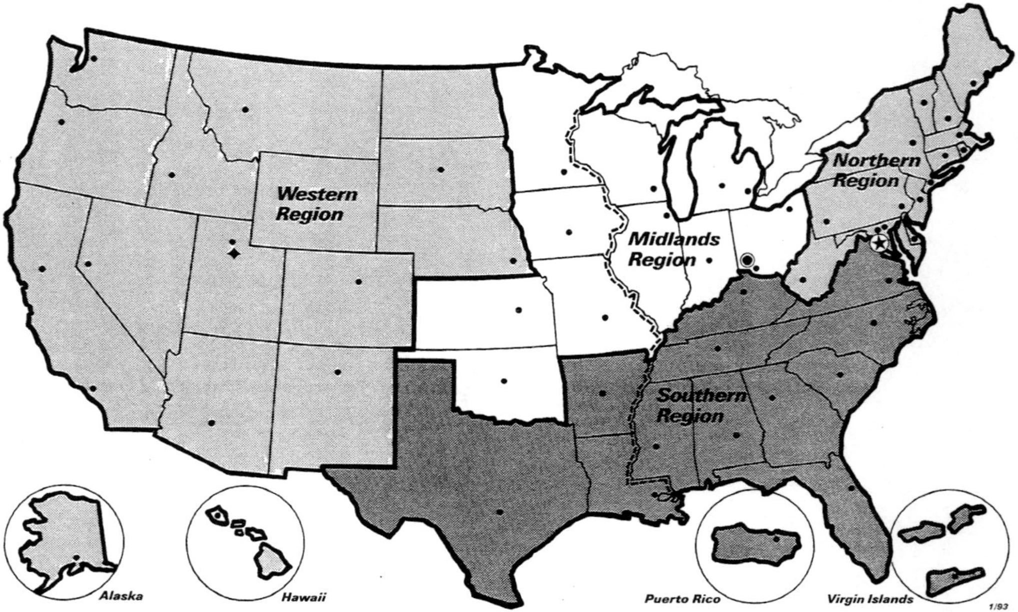

FIGURE 7.3

Library Service Network

orientations and tours. The incumbent serves as an advisor to the director and assists in identifying appropriate program modifications.

The Inventory Management Section is responsible for controlling the national inventory, storage, retrieval, and handling of materials used in the NLS/BPH program; distributing equipment, furnishings, and other items delivered to NLS/BPH; monitoring, coordinating, and evaluating the activities of two multistate centers; maintaining a procedures manual for use by the multistate centers and a supplies catalog for use by network libraries; and supervising and evaluating book redistribution procedures.

The Music Section is responsible for developing, maintaining, circulating, and promoting the use of national collections in the field of music, including the collection of large-print books about music and musicians, music scores, and instructional methods, and other special format music materials on cassette, disc, and in braille. Further responsibilities include providing access to music periodicals; developing and maintaining a noncirculating print reference collection of books about music and musicians; and encouraging the development of new techniques and materials for teaching music to blind and physically handicapped individuals.

The Network Services Section is responsible for coordinating national network activities, including both responding to inquiries about services and coordinating responses to network inquiries; directing the interlibrary loan programs; providing consultant services to identify problem patterns and to evaluate performance in relation to established standards; compiling bibliographies of special media materials; organizing the orientation program for network participants; maintaining a procedures manual for use by network libraries; and providing library service to U.S. citizens living outside the United States.

The Reference Section is responsible for providing to network libraries, other professional groups, and the general public a national reference and referral service on blindness and physical handicaps, except in the fields of medicine and law. Additional duties are providing special and general reference services to the staff of NLS/BPH; developing a collection of print materials on blindness and physical handicaps to support the activities described above; maintaining records and preparing statistical reports on network activities and program developments; coordinating an automated mailing list incorporating data on readers, libraries, and organizations; and providing consultant services on volunteer programs in network libraries.

SUMMARY

In short the National Library Service for the Blind and Physically Handicapped is managed in a manner which is designed to involve all professional staff, and as many of the clerical and administrative staff as wish and are able to participate. It is a consumer-driven organization with a service philosophy embodied in Arthur Ransome's classic guiding principle: "Grab a chance and you won't be sorry for a might have been."

STATISTICAL INFORMATION

Sponsor:	Library of Congress
Name of Unit:	National Library Service for the Blind and Physically Handicapped
Location:	1291 Taylor Street, NW Washington, DC 20542
Name of Head of Unit:	Frank Kurt Cylke
Title of Head of Unit:	Director
Title of Immediate Supervisor:	Associate Librarian for National Programs
Staff Size:	119
Main Subjects Collected:	Bestsellers, Biographies, Fiction, Health, How-To Books, Music, Religion, Science, Science Fiction, Sports

Collection Size:

Books:	153,000
Copies:	16,000,000
Current subscriptions:	70

Special Collections:	Spanish Language Materials, Children's Literature, Young Adult Fiction

Computer Services: NLS Net

Readership: 764,800
(FY1993)

Circulation: 21,826,000
(FY1993)

Regional Libraries: 56

Subregional Libraries: 87

Multistate Centers: 2

Appropriations: $45.3 million (FY93)

Chapter 8
National Library of Medicine
Kent A. Smith
Robert Mehnert

The United States National Library of Medicine (NLM) had its beginnings in 1836 when a small library was established in the office of the Surgeon General of the U.S. Army. In the autumn of 1864, an Army Surgeon, John Shaw Billings, was given the temporary assignment of putting into order this small collection of books and journals.

When Billings finally finished his "temporary" assignment and retired in 1895, that office collection had become the largest, most complete body of medical literature anywhere in the world. In 1956, by act of Congress, the institution was named the National Library of Medicine and placed in the Public Health Service of the Department of Health, Education, and Welfare. The collection today numbers approximately five million items. It and the staff of 600, are housed in the Library's two modern buildings on the campus of the National Institutes of Health in Bethesda, Maryland (see Photo 8.1). Table 8.1 lists various statistics pertaining to workloads and resources.

Access to this immense collection has always been a primary concern of the Library (see Photo 8.2). NLM's most well-known print product, the monthly bibliography *Index Medicus*, begun by Billings in 1879, is still published today and is used by health professionals around the world. Some 3,000 journals in 40 languages are regularly indexed.

THE NATIONAL NETWORK

In the United States, a formal National Network of Libraries of Medicine, supported by the NLM, has systematized the efficient

Photo 8.1. The National Library of Medicine has two buildings on the campus of the National Institutes of Health in Bethesda, Maryland. The main library building (right) was dedicated in 1962; the 10-story Lister Hill Center, containing offices, communications laboratories, and computer facilities, was dedicated in 1980. Courtesy of the National Library of Medicine.

TABLE 8.1. Selected Statistics*

Collection (book and nonbook)	4,970,000
Serial titles received	22,400
Articles indexed for MEDLINE	376,000
Circulation requests filled	401,000
For interlibrary loan	220,000
For onsite users	181,000
Computerized searches (all databases)	5,964,000
Appropriation	$103,613,000
Full-time staff	596

*For the year ending September 30, 1993

sharing of library resources among health science institutions. There are 4,000 members of the Network, including hospitals, medical schools, academic institutions, private companies, and government agencies. The National Library of Medicine serves as a backstop to the Network, supplying materials not easily available elsewhere.

There are several ways in which the NLM assists members of the Network, including contracts with eight major institutions that serve as Regional Medical Libraries and several programs of grant and contract support for hospitals and other institutions. This support may be used to connect health institutions to national information sources (including the Internet), conduct outreach programs in local communities, provide new information resources and services to an institution's health professionals, or develop large-scale integrated advanced information systems. The NLM also funds

Photo 8.2. A partial view of the Main Reading Room of the National Library of Medicine, which seats 100 and is open to the public. The historical collections are served by a separate reading room. Courtesy of the National Library of Medicine.

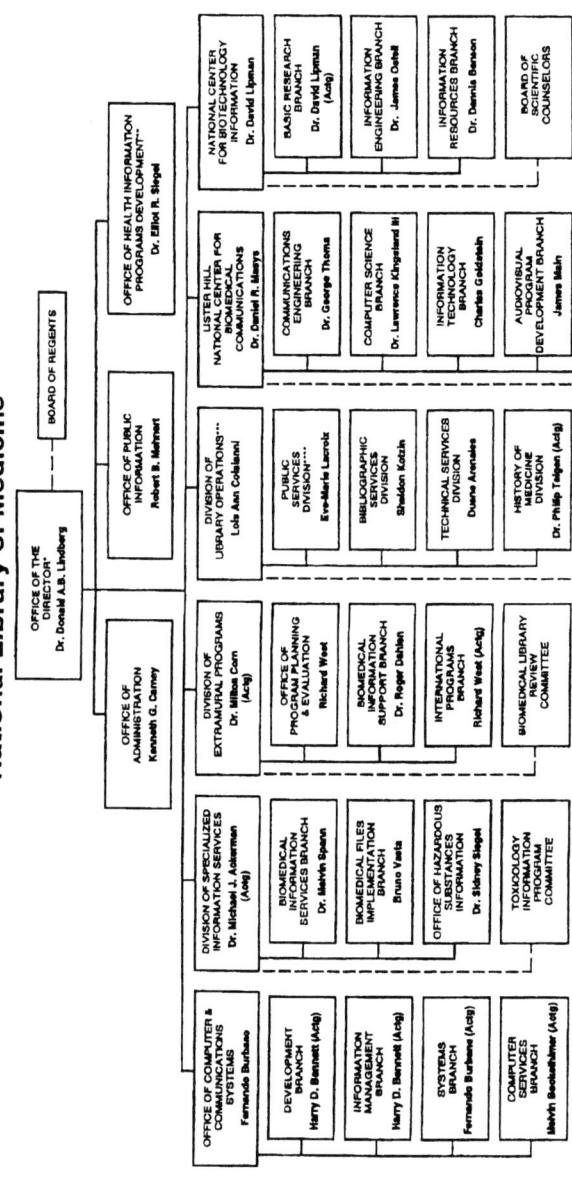

133

DEPARTMENT OF HEALTH AND HUMAN SERVICES
Public Health Service
National Institutes of Health

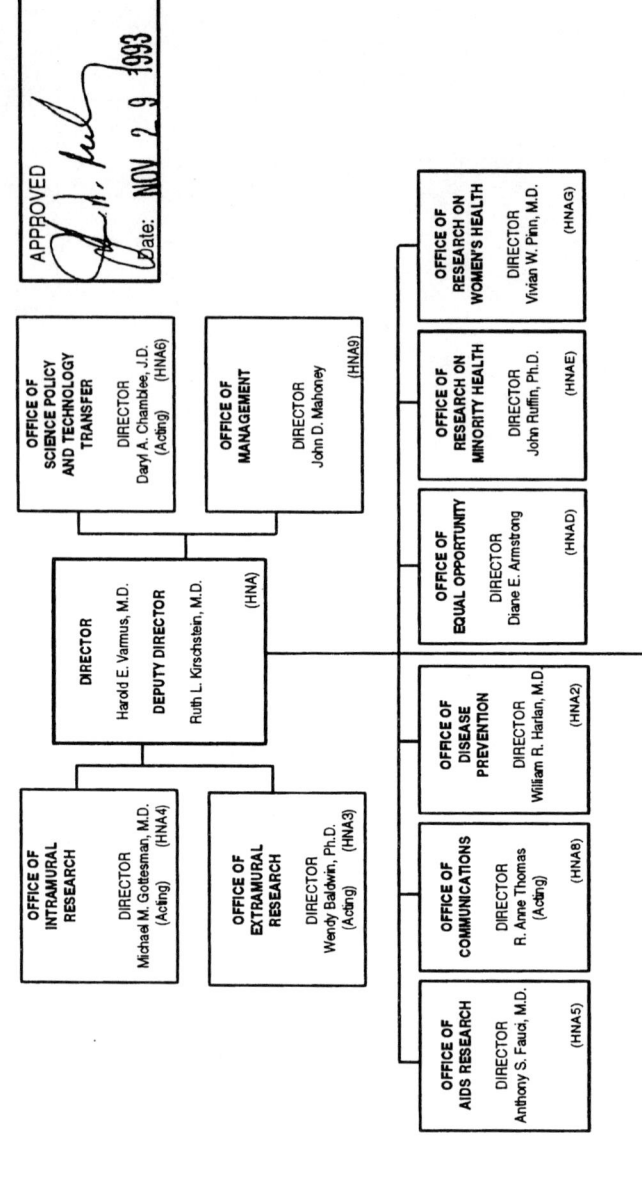

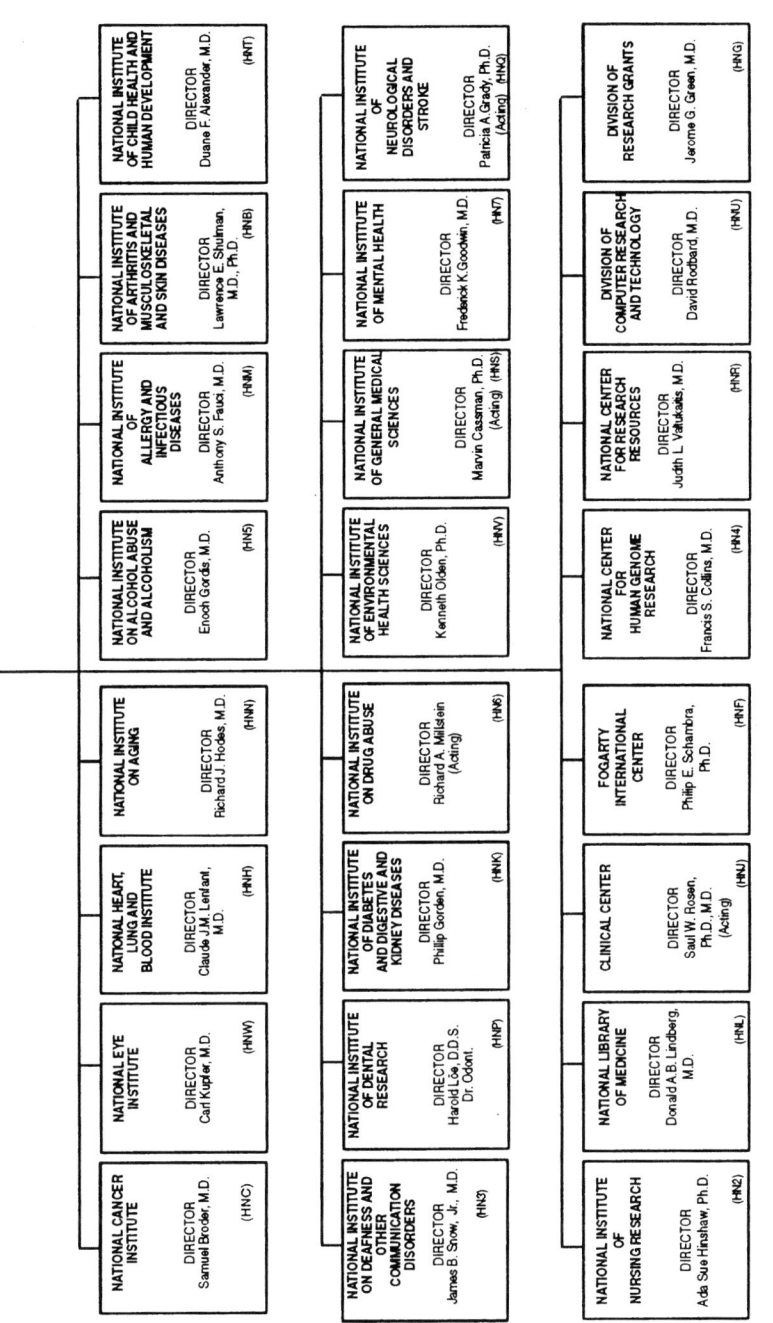

Source: U.S. Public Health Service, Public Information Office

research and training in "medical informatics" through a grant program.

COMPUTERIZED BIBLIOGRAPHIC ACCESS

NLM's MEDLARS (Medical Literature Analysis and Retrieval System) is recognized as the first major computerized bibliographic database in the biosciences. It was developed and introduced by the Library in 1964 primarily as a method of producing the *Index Medicus*.

MEDLARS still produces the *Index Medicus* (and other printed bibliographies), but today it is perhaps better known as the source of a family of some 40 online databases that together contain almost 15 million records. MEDLINE (MEDLARS online), searchable since 1971, was the first of these databases. It contains all the *Index Medicus* references (and additional citations from nursing and dentistry) from 1966 to the present–more than seven million records in all. MEDLINE is currently growing at the rate of almost 400,000 references a year.

Most of NLM's databases, like MEDLINE, are bibliographic in nature. Examples are AIDSLINE, BIOETHICSLINE, HEALTH PLANNING AND ADMINISTRATION, and CANCERLIT. Several databases, however, contain factual information. The Hazardous Substances Data Bank (HSDB), intended for use by emergency personnel responding to chemical spills or other environmental crises, is one of these. Another is the Toxic Chemical Release Inventory database which provides specific information about the release of chemicals into the air, ground, and water in the U.S. These and several other specialized databases are on the Library's TOXNET system.

Access to the Library's online retrieval network has grown dramatically in recent years. The databases on NLM's computers may now be accessed by some 60,000 individuals and organizations in the U.S. and in other countries, including medical and other schools of the health professions, hospitals, private firms, and government agencies. In 1993 this network accounted for almost six million searches.

The primary reason for the extraordinarily rapid growth of the system in recent years is the widespread adoption of Grateful Med. Grateful Med is a program for personal computers, developed by the NLM, that facilitates convenient and inexpensive access to the Library's major databases. Rare is the American health professional who doesn't have access to a microcomputer in the office, laboratory, or home. This and a telephone are all that are required to put one directly in touch with MEDLINE and most other NLM databases.

Grateful Med expands the options of health professionals who require access to the literature. Medical libraries, of course, continue to provide sophisticated and comprehensive database search services; but health professionals who do not have convenient access to a library (for example, rural physicians) now can conduct their own searches. In 1992 NLM added document ordering capability (known as Loansome Doc) to Grateful Med.

NLM's databases are also available internationally. Users in some countries come online directly to the NLM. MEDLARS partners in other countries have put NLM databases on their own computers and provide online retrieval in their own and, in some cases, neighboring countries. In addition, commercial vendors of databases, such as Dialog and BRS, lease certain NLM databases and provide access to the users of their networks. Also, a number of private companies offer MEDLINE on compact disks (CD-ROM). Through this variety of arrangements NLM's databases are widely available to health professionals in this country and around the world.

MANAGEMENT PLANNING

In January 1987 the National Library of Medicine published an ambitious Long Range Plan to guide the institution into the twenty-first century. The impetus for this plan came from the Library's Director, Donald A. B. Lindberg, MD, who, from the time of his assumption of the position in August 1984, saw the need for such a plan as a high priority. The NLM Board of Regents enthusiastically endorsed the concept and agreed that the plan should be produced under its aegis. More than 100 leaders in medicine, librarianship, academia, government, and industry participated and contributed their skills and advice to the planning process in the form of panel discussions.

The Long Range Plan consists of an executive summary, a one-volume report with detailed recommendations, and reports of the deliberations and findings of the five panels.[1] The panels covered the principal domains of the NLM: building the collection, providing access to the biomedical literature, factual databases, medical informatics, and health professions education. The experts' advice was distilled into some 50 discrete recommendations; the additional staff and budgetary resources required to implement the recommendations were also included.

The NLM Long Range Plan has not suffered the fate of many such plans–a place of honor on the administrator's shelf. The Library's entire budget has been recast in the functional terms specified within the plan, and one can see at a glance how the NLM is actually apportioning its resources to meet the goals of the plan. NLM's functional budget in essence becomes its short range operational plan. It is a simple matter to refer in the budget to functional areas such as reference, document delivery, hazardous substance information, and medical informatics, to mention just a few, and to see how the various activities are faring in the competition for money and staff. This approach is in contrast to the more usual "line-item" or "object class" budgetary technique.

Such functional budgeting data also becomes a ready source for internal management information systems. Regular monthly reporting mechanisms, be they manual or automated, contain comparative data to provide top management with workload trends and productivity measurements.

The planning recommendations have had a direct and beneficial impact on the Library. This can be seen most clearly in several new NLM activities that have come about as a direct result of the plan: the National Center for Biotechnology Information, electronic imaging, and outreach.

Several recommendations concerned the need for an organization to handle the massive amount of biotechnology information being generated by the National Institutes of Health's Human Genome Program and other research in molecular biology. Such a program would create sophisticated databases containing molecular genetic information and the advanced software needed to access this information. This recommendation found a vigorous champion in the late Senator Claude Pepper, and, as a result of his work, legislation to create the National Center for Biotechnology Information within the Library was signed into law in November 1988.

The initiative on electronic imaging also derives directly from a recommendation of the Long Range Plan. In this case, the Lister Hill National Center for Biomedical Communications, a research component of the NLM, took the lead in organizing an advisory panel. The panel, agreeing with the general recommendation about the need to establish a "biomedical images library" at the NLM, went a step further and recommended specifically that the Library undertake a "Visible Human" project–to create, in complete and minute anatomical detail, three-dimensional representations of the male and female human body. Such a computerized dataset could have great benefit in medical research, education, and practice. Their advice was codified in a report[2] that was accepted by the Board of Regents and that is now, with the assistance of contractors, being implemented by the Library.

The Library has had a program for some 25 years to develop information services in toxicology, pharmacology, and environmental health. Because these subjects continue to be of great concern to society, a Planning Panel of experts was appointed by the Board of Regents to examine these services. Their report contained a number of recommendations, and an implementation plan is now being drawn up.

Topics that will be the object of future planning efforts are training for medical librarians and the Library's international role as a center for medical information.

OUTREACH

The planning advisers noted that one area–outreach–was worthy of additional consideration. The basis for their concern was the belief that the Library's services were not being fully utilized because many health professionals did not know of the existence of such services as MEDLINE and Grateful Med. Especially those serving in rural and otherwise underserved areas of the country would find them to be of great benefit.

To consider how to address this problem, the Board of Regents named an Outreach Planning Panel and appointed as its chairman noted surgeon Dr. Michael E. DeBakey. The Panel delivered to the Library in August 1989 a report[3] that recommended a wide-ranging program of outreach activities that is now being implemented. The functional category "outreach" is an important component of the budget of every NLM program. This is an example of how the original long range plan not only functioned as a road map, identifying outreach as a destination, but also served as a mechanism for setting in motion this significant initiative.

Outreach is more than an individual program: the mandate to improve health professionals' access to information is inherent in the Library's fundamental mission and cuts across NLM organizational lines. Outreach as a special initiative provides a focal point for a broad range of activities that are intended to ensure that health professionals are aware of and have access to the latest scientific findings in an easy-to-use form.

The Office of Health Information Programs Development was created within the NLM Office of the Director in 1992. The new office contains three units: the Office of Outreach Development, the Office of Planning and Analysis, and the Office of International Programs. The Office of Outreach Development will plan, develop, and evaluate the Library's outreach programs and will serve as a catalyst, addressing new opportunities for outreach activities throughout the NLM. To this end, an interdivisional Outreach Coordinating Committee has also been established.

The NLM outreach program relies heavily on cooperative efforts with the member institutions of the National Network of Libraries of Medicine. NLM has initiated more than 100 outreach projects since the publication of the DeBakey report. Many have as their goal the training of physicians and other health professionals to use Grateful Med, with an emphasis on libraries in rural and inner city areas.

With the advantage of several years' experience, NLM is now seeking to discover what can be learned from the completed projects, and what changes, if any, should be made in the future. A recent NLM staff evaluation of 30 Grateful Med outreach projects conducted between 1990 and 1992 will provide guidance for refining and improving this type of outreach activity. Systematic evaluation will continue to be an important component of outreach, to identify and document those strategies that have been effective and those that have been found wanting, and to share these experiences with current and future collaborators who will benefit from this knowledge in the course of undertaking new outreach initiatives.

RESEARCH AND DEVELOPMENT

The NLM engages in cutting-edge communications research and development through two major components–the Lister Hill National Center for Biomedical Communications, and the National Center for Biotechnology Information. These organizations conduct a variety of investigations, both in-house and collaborative, in such areas as expert systems, digital imaging, the development of a Unified Medical Language System, and the creation of databases and sophisticated software for molecular biology.

The original long range plan strongly supported the Library's research and development programs. What it could not have foreseen was the surge of bipartisan high-level support since 1991 for a concept called High Performance Computing and Communications (HPCC). Public Law 102-192, the High Performance Computing and Communications Act of 1991, sponsored by then-Senator Albert Gore and Representative George E. Brown Jr. (D-CA), provided impetus to a corollary Presidential initiative in this area.

NLM's research and development programs stand to benefit from the new initiative, including the National Research and Education Network that is a vital part of the program. NLM is the focal point within the Department of Health and Human Services for undertaking the biomedical component of the initiative. Dr. Lindberg has been appointed by the White House Office of Science and Technology Policy to a concurrent position as head of the National Coordination Office for High Performance Computing and Communications.

President Clinton and Vice President Gore, in their economic growth package for America, have reemphasized the importance of the nation's information infrastructure. Their report states that, "Just as the interstate highway system marked a historical turning point in our commerce, today 'information superhighway'–able to move ideas, data, and images around the country and around the world–are critical to American competitiveness and economic strength."[4]

High-performance computers and high-speed computer networks are key technologies for the future of biomedical science. Grand challenges in biomedicine, such as the analysis of the human genome, prediction of biological structure and function from genetic code, and rational drug design, will require new and faster computers, advanced software, a high-speed National Research and Education Network, and expanded training of scientists in the use of computer-based tools. NLM sees its role as ensuring that American medical scientists and health care professionals have access to the world of biomedical information that will be made accessible through the higher performance computing technology and high-speed network resulting from the initiative.

Specifically, the Library, through its Lister Hill Center, will be able to proceed with the "Visible Human" project described earlier. New technologies developed under the initiative will result in the ability to compute, display, and transmit the enormous amount of digital information that comprise complicated images of the human body at millimeter-level resolution. The availability of such a tool would have enormous implications for medical education, research, and practice.

Second, the Library will itself develop sophisticated connections to the evolving high-speed research network. We envision that our PC-based software, Grateful Med, will be the route of choice for many scientists and health professionals in accessing databases via the National Research and Education Network (NREN). Of course, the NREN will have profound implications for *all* libraries, not just those serving the health sciences.

Third, the Library will accelerate development of the Unified Medical Language System (UMLS). Begun by NLM in 1986, the Unified Medical Language System project is a research and development effort designed to help health care practitioners and researchers to locate, retrieve, and integrate useful information that is distributed among disparate machine-readable sources. The sources of interest include bibliographic databases, patient record systems, factual databases, and knowledge-based expert systems. The barriers to integrated access to these sources include the many different ways the same biomedical concepts are expressed in different sources and by different users, and the sheer number and variety of databases and systems that contain useful biomedical information. A number of prototype UMLS-related products are now being tested around the country.

And, finally, the Library, through its National Center for Biotechnology Information, will continue to implement the GenInfo suite of biotechnology-related databases to provide investigators with a vital tool for scientific discovery. Database searching is being made available to genome centers over high-speed datalinks, and new retrieval methods are being developed that require supercomputer processor speeds and massive amounts of memory.

While clearly the Administration will continue to enhance the basic research components of the HPCC initiative–those that deal with high-speed gigabit networks and massively parallel computers–the new emphasis will be on practical applications, including those for health care. In the foreseeable future it will not be unusual for physicians in rural America to consult with specialists in major medical centers by transmitting, in "real time," medical images and other patient data over high-speed lines.

As a library, the National Library of Medicine is certainly atypical. It is, in fact, unique. Nevertheless, the challenges NLM is now facing–and grappling with–will soon enough confront all libraries. Communications and information technology may be viewed with suspicion and trepidation by some; at NLM it is seen as the only means by which health professionals will be able to keep abreast of the continuing growth in scientific information.

NOTES

1. National Library of Medicine. 1987. *Long range plan: report of the NLM Board of Regents*. Bethesda, MD: National Library of Medicine, January.
2. National Library of Medicine. 1990. *Electronic imaging: report of the Board of Regents*. Bethesda, MD: National Library of Medicine, April.

3. National Library of Medicine. 1989. *Improving health professionals' access to information: report of the Board of Regents.* Bethesda, MD: National Library of Medicine, August.

4. *Technology for America's Economic Growth, A New Direction to Build Economic Strength.* 1993. President William J. Clinton, Vice President Albert Gore, Jr. February 22, p. 28.

STATISTICAL INFORMATION

Sponsor: U.S. Public Health Service, National Institutes of Health

Name of Unit: National Library of Medicine

Location: 8600 Rockville Pike
Bethesda, Maryland 20894

Name of Head of Unit: Donald A. B. Lindberg, MD

Title of Head of Unit: Director

Staff Size: 596

Main Subjects Collected: Biomedicine, Health and Health Care, Medical Technology, Medicine, Public Health, Toxicology

Collection Size:

Books:	906,217
Current subscriptions:	22,397
Bound journal volumes:	998,464
Microfilm:	58,484
Microfiche:	266,998
Pamphlets:	172,021
Manuscripts:	2,454,542
Pictures:	56,600
Audiovisuals:	55,736
Software:	649
Total:	4,969,711

Special Collections: History of Medicine

Computer Services:	MEDLARS, MEDLINE, CATLINE, AIDSLINE, AVLINE, CANCERLIT, POPLINE, SDILINE, SERLINE, TOXLINE
Articles Indexed for Medline:	376,312
Computer Searches (All Databases):	5,964,000
Circulation Requests Filled: (FY1993)	401,162
Interlibrary Loan:	220,464
For On-site Users:	180,698
Appropriation:	$103,613,000

PART VI: CONCLUSIONS

Chapter 9

An Overview of Effective Management in Federal Libraries

Charles D. Missar

In the foregoing chapters, seven library managers have discussed the ways in which they carry out their programs and responsibilities in very different settings. From the large national libraries to smaller, very specialized facilities there are basic procedures in library management that must be followed and adapted to particular locations. It will be the purpose of this chapter to present an overview and wrap-up of management procedures usually associated with federal facilities, but some of which might be applied to the full range of libraries.

By now it should be evident that the manager of a federally sponsored library has many responsibilities, not the least of which is to direct an efficient and effective facility. This requires dealing with people, places, and things (resources and equipment) in a professional manner. There are various ways this can be done, and each of the previous chapters has explained in detail how it was accomplished in seven very different facilities. Now it is time to take an overview of all these responsibilities and activities.

It is obvious that the manager should be a people-oriented person because of the number of roles that he or she must play in relating to staff, administration, patrons, visitors, contractors, and vendors.

Most important is the role regarding the library staff, since it is as an organizer, motivator, decision-maker, and especially as a leader that the library manager can be most effective. The need for planning and organizing an efficient operation cannot be underestimated. This requires a detailed knowledge of library operations and an insight into ways to make it function smoothly. Once the best organizational structure is in place, it is necessary to motivate the staff to carry out the plans and activities in a timely and orderly fashion. If staff has been involved in some of the planning, they may be more interested in cooperating in the operation.

If and when problems develop, it makes sense to address them immediately and make decisions that are reasonable and proper, based upon facts and not assumptions. Suggestions and comments from staff should be encouraged and acted upon as appropriate. This can lead to greater cooperation.

However, as a good leader, the manager must take the initiative to lead the way and guide the staff to accomplish its work in a timely manner. This requires skill in supervision and direction. The work needs to be explained clearly to the staff and then monitored consistently to insure that the tasks are done completely and correctly. Ideally, it is also essential to have the right people in the right places. Here again it is the manager's responsibility to select individuals with the background, training, experience, and disposition for the tasks at hand. This is not always possible in a federal setting, because personnel are not always selected with the consent of the manager. Frequently they are already in place with some job-security rights, and at other times personnel are reassigned at the direction of higher management. Then it is incumbent for the manager to evaluate the personalities and skills of the individuals so that they can be assigned to tasks most relevant to their interests and abilities.

Often it is necessary to recommend training to improve and enhance employee's skills. This must be done with fairness–giving equal opportunities to all employees so that they cannot charge discrimination or favoritism which, in turn, might affect future pay increases or promotions.

A major responsibility of library managers is the evaluation of employees, which requires special knowledge, ability, and skill. Various employee evaluation programs have been developed to afford fair and reasonably objective judgment about performance. Usually the agency selects the plan and develops the guidelines and procedures. One of the more recent approaches is to have the employee, in conjunction with the supervisor, develop a set of job-specific tasks to be accomplished during the coming year. Mutually agreed upon goals are set with appropriate deadlines. Both parties then approve and sign the agreement. As performance reviews are made during the year, the employee will be expected to report on progress. The supervisor will note this and make comments on the quality and quantity of work performed related to the goals. At the end of the year the manager will give a final evaluation based upon the level of performance and the employee's effectiveness in meeting the agreed upon goals within the required deadlines. A quality rating of outstanding, superior, satisfactory, or unsatisfactory is given. This rating will be used to determine awards, pay increases, and future promotions. If there is disagreement, the employee has the right to appeal this decision.

The manager is also in the role of employee with his or her supervisor. A similar type of performance agreement is worked out between the two with tasks, goals, and deadlines. Depending upon their working relationship it can be a fairly routine procedure for the supervisor to have full confidence in the manager and support the planned goals presented. It can also be a very difficult matter, if the library is being micromanaged from above. Then there can be considerable stress and strain over goals, objectives, and deadlines. It then becomes imperative to work out compromises for the good of the organization and the staff.

Another area where the manager has to deal with many people is administrative services, namely: personnel, budget, finance, contracts, and legal matters. Each of these sections are service areas which support and assist the library in carrying out its mission. Unless the library is a large, self-contained unit such as one of the national libraries, it generally does not have its own service units. Therefore it is dependent on specialists in the various areas to provide the required support. The manager must deal with these people in a congenial manner to obtain their full cooperation. For example, in a hiring case, the librarian in charge develops a list of duties for the new position. The personnel unit then formalizes the position description, classifies the job as to grade level and pay status, advertises the position, and recruits suitable candidates. The manager interviews the individuals and makes the final selection. The personnel people will then make the offer to the person, and if it is accepted, will make the arrangements to bring the person in as a full-fledged employee.

The manager also has frequent occasions to work with the budget staff to be sure that finance plans are in line with agency funding and that expenditures are on target for the fiscal year. With the finance unit it is important to see that approved bills are paid promptly and that disagreements are resolved quickly. The contracts unit assists with certain types of procurements for books, periodicals, equipment, and a variety of library services which are obtained through other federal agencies or from the private sector. It is good for the manager to explain exactly what is needed so that the contracts staff can arrange for these products and services with a minimum of difficulty.

Finally, there will be occasions when the manager will need legal advice about some problems or actions from copyright matters to grievances and discrimination. It helps when the manager knows the legal staff and is able to speak frankly with them to get the required professional advice and support.

In addition to the above mentioned people, the manager also interacts with library patrons and visitors, including vendors. Depending on staff size, most of the activities with patrons are handled by staff members who are professionally trained to assist and direct users. Only when problems develop or special help is needed will the manager become involved. As the person in charge, it will be the manager's responsibility to resolve difficulties or to offer assistance as a last resort.

Since visitors vary greatly in their needs, their importance, and their prior knowledge of a subject, usually only those who require special attention will be the manager's concern. Ordinarily the staff should be able to provide the necessary information. The same would be true of vendors who visit the library. If they are discussing a specific product, the staff member most knowledgeable will meet with them. Only when it is in the manager's interest would he or she be involved.

A somewhat recent phenomenon which has come to federal libraries is the "contracting-out" of all or part of the operation. It is required that a technical representative, who is a federal employee, serve as a liaison between the government and the contractor. This employee does not supervise the contract employees, which is not allowed, but handles work-related matters and not personnel problems. Conversely, federal employees cannot be supervised by contractors. In libraries where all operations are done under contract, the library manager is usually a contract employee and the technical representative represents the government from outside the library. In facilities where only a portion of the work is done under contract, the technical representative is either the manager or an assistant. Certainly in such instances there is no problem for the manager or any other federal employee to discuss work with contractors, but it is important that suggestions, changes, or problems connected with the work be channeled through the technical representative.

The physical aspects of the library are also of considerable importance to the manager. Its geographic location is usually selected by the General Services Administration in conjunction with the head of the federal agency involved. In theory, the physical space assigned to the library is negotiable. However, because of the size and weight of the collection and equipment, there are often only a limited number of locations in the building where it can be placed. Once that decision has been made, the arrangement of staff offices, reading areas, and the position of shelving, files, and equipment is ordinarily left to the library manager and staff to work out. Occasionally if the budget permits, professional library planners are called in to help and advise.

It should be remembered that the library fills many needs. It is a reading area, a study facility, a research source, a "circle of knowledge" and idea exchange, a meeting place for discussions, and occasionally a social site. It is truly a dynamic entity, ever growing and changing. In order for it to meet all of these needs, the manger must be ever aware of its capabilities and potential, and transmit these to other employees in the agency.

Since a library is ever growing, it is essential to plan for expansion for books, periodicals, pamphlets, and microforms. Space is also needed for new equipment and systems as new technologies become part of the library's resources. Frequently, as budgets allow and services require, additional staff space may be needed. Thus room for expansion should be built into the library's plans from the start, so that it is not necessary to make unexpected moves or extensive shifting every few years.

The manager must also be aware of the safety of the staff and the security of the collection. Employees deserve to feel safe in their work space–protected from violence, fire, or hazards of any type. Telephones and intercoms are essential for alerting superiors of potential problems as well as for convenient communication. Fire alarms and smoke detectors need to be widespread and in working order.

Security for the collection and equipment is also of critical importance. Since materials of historical or archival value must be carefully protected, closed stack areas or secured rooms may be necessary. Some kind of security system for all materials available for use in the library or for outside circulation is essential, including magnetic strips in each book and periodical. This is one way to demonstrate that management is really concerned about safeguarding its property. Many federal libraries have detectors at entrances and exits, require sign-in and -out sheets at the door, and issue badges to visitors.

All equipment should be marked with a property label, especially expensive portable computers and typewriters, which may even need to be secured to desks or walls to protect them from being stolen. A comprehensive plan for the safety and security of the place should be a part of the overall management policy. Today many of the federal libraries also have a disaster plan.

In spite of this need for security it is essential to make the facility as attractive, inviting, and comfortable as possible with decorations of various kinds. Appropriate photographs, paintings, and hangings can help to enliven the walls, while plants and display cases can be used effectively to divide up interior space. The manager should be concerned that the physical facilities will attract individuals to come to use the library and will allow people to find it a place conducive for official and personal reading and research.

Finally, the manger must be concerned about "things" in the library. In the past 50 or 60 years the library has changed from a place with just books, periodicals, pamphlets, and newspapers to a treasure trove of all kinds of resources and equipment. First came technical reports followed quickly by reels of microfilm with film readers and printers. Then room had to be made for microfiche cabinets with fiche-to-fiche duplicators and random-access microfiche readers/printers. With the introduction of computer technology, punched cards and computer tapes appeared, which were followed by remote consoles connected by telephone lines to random-access storage devices. These quickly paved the way for the online interactive bibliographic utilities and the library's need for computer terminals with video screens, keyboards, modems, and printers. While these computer terminals were being upgraded, the personal computers (PCs) appeared with multiple applications and software programs to assist in library record keeping for circulation, ordering, periodical checking, etc.–the integrated library system was born! More recently the compact disk, with its CD-ROM readers and printers, has brought another new technology into the library. And videocassettes with their VCR players and cameras with audio recordings make multimedia presentations possible. Networking has further extended the library's access to information, and now the Internet has literally opened up the world's library collections.

The federal library, as well as libraries in general, has indeed become a treasure trove of individuals, resources, and equipment for the Information Age. A good manager not only needs to be aware of what the facility can offer, but also needs to promote and make it available to a highly educated and skilled user group, a challenge which will continue well into the future.

Bibliography

Adkinson, Burton W. 1978. *Two Centuries of Federal Information.* Stroudsburg, PA: Dowden, Hutchinson and Ross.

Bellassai, Marcia C. 1983. *Survey of Federal Libraries, Fiscal Year 1978.* Washington, DC: National Center for Education Statistics.

Benton, Mildred. 1973. *Federal Library Resources.* New York: Science Associates/International.

――― and Signe Ottersen. 1970. *Roster of Federal Libraries.* Washington, DC: The George Washington University Medical Center.

Berger, Patricia W. and Cerutti, Elsie. 1980. The management of online reference search services in federal libraries. *Science & Technology Libraries.* 1(1): 81-107; Fall.

Bond, Marvin A. 1984. Planning, budgeting and personnel management in a scientific library of the federal government: National Bureau of Standards. *Science & Technology Libraries.* 4(3/4): 45-60; Spring/Summer.

Comptroller General of the United States. 1973. *Report to the Congress: Review of Federal Library Operations in Metropolitan Washington, DC.* Washington, DC: General Accounting Office.

Cylke, Frank Kurt. 1972. *Federal Libraries.* Washington, DC: Federal Library Committee.

Donohue, Joseph C. 1987. *The Future of Federal Libraries and Information Centers.* Washington, DC: Federal Library and Information Center Committee.

Evans, Luther H. 1968. *Federal Departmental Libraries: A Summary Report of a Survey and a Conference.* Washington, DC: U.S. Department of Health, Education and Welfare.

Evinger, William R. 1993. *Directory of Federal Libraries.* 2d ed. Phoenix, AZ: Oryx Press.

Federal Libraries in the 21st Century: Changing Roles in the Elec-

tronic Age. Summary Report on Conference Proceedings. 1993. Washington, DC: Federal Library and Information Center Committee.

The Federal Library Mission: A Statement of Principles and Guidelines. 1966. Washington, DC: Federal Library Committee.

Federal Library Resources. 1984. New York: Science Associates/International.

Kadec, Sarah Thomas and Watts, Carol B. 1988. Scientific and technical libraries in the federal government: one hundred years of service. In: *One Hundred Years of Sci-tech Libraries: A Brief History.* Edited by Ellis Mount. Binghamton, NY: Haworth Press, 35-49.

Strauss, William. 1968. *Guide to Laws and Regulations on Federal Libraries.* New York: Bowker.

Survey of Federal Libraries, Fiscal Year 1972. 1972. Washington, DC: U.S. Department of Health, Education and Welfare, Education Division.

Survey of Special Libraries Serving the Federal Government. 1968. Washington, DC: U.S. Department of Health, Education and Welfare, Office of Education.

Index

Administrative Office of the U.S.
  Courts
  automation policies, 41-42
  circuit library support, 38
  Computer Assisted Legal
    Reference services (CALR),
    38-39
  Human Resources Division, 41
  Integrated Technology Division,
    41-42
  Lawbook Section, 39-40
  Legal Research and Library
    Program office (LRLB),
    36,38-39
  space design, and management, 41
  U.S. Courts Design Guide, 41
American Library Association
  Armed Forces Librarian's
    Roundtable (AFLRT), 58
  Federal Librarian's Roundtable
    (FLRT), 58
Army. *See* U.S. Army headings,
  military headings, Pentagon
  library, U.S. Department
  of Defense, Redstone
  Scientific Information Center
Army Librarian Career Program,
  59-60
Army Library Committee
  cooperative projects, 59
  implementation of, 59
Army Library Institute, annual
  training program, 59-60,68
Army Library Listserv (ALL), U.S.
  Military Academy, 60
Army Library Management Office,
  59

Bibliographic databases, 136
Book selection, 92,110
Budget. *See* entries under individual
  libraries

Catholic University of America, 68
CD-ROM products. *See* entries
  under individual libraries
Circulation service, 23,65
Collection development. *See* entries
  under individual libraries
Computerized catalogs, 23,77
Congressional Research Service
  (CRS), 21,26

Defense Library on Disc, 67

Effective management, overview,
  149-155
EGAL (Electronic Gateway to Army
  Libraries), 60

Federal Circuit library system.
  See also Sixth Circuit Library
  System
  book procurement, 39
  budget decisions, 42
  common features, 36
  courts served, 38
  databases accessed, 39
  decentralized environment, 48-49
  direct ordering of research
    materials, 40

159

Federal Circuit library system, *(continued)*
  establishment of, 36
  integrated library system planned, 39
  interaction with judges, 49
  lawbook ordering, 39
  local library funds, 39-40
  local policy formulation, 49
  local service variations, 48
  national service contracts, 38-39
  organizational structure, 35
  pay schedules, 40
  regional jurisdiction, 38
  satellite libraries, 38,48
  staffing patterns, 36
  staffing related to judges served, 38
  statutory requirements, 36
  system-wide policy, 49
Federal libraries
  case studies, 6
  collection development, 1
  contracting-out for services, 152
  effective management, 149-155
  information services, 1-2
  management procedures, 149
  public services, 1
  scope, 2
  space utilization, 153
  statistical breakdown, 3-4
  systems specialist, 1-2
  technical services, 1
  types, 5
Federal Library and Information Center Committee (FLICC), 25,39,62,68,100
Federal library manager
  administrative contacts, 151
  budget and finance contacts, 152
  collection management, 154-155
  contract employees, 153
  leadership role, 150
  legal contacts, 152
  library appearance, 154

Federal library manager *(continued)*
  organizational influences, 2
  patron interactions, 152
  personnel actions, 151
  personnel evaluation procedures, 150-151
  property protection, 154
  responsibilities, 149
  role of, 149
  security considerations, 154
  space management, 153
  staff assignment, 150
  staff involvement, 150
  staff safety, 154
  staff training, 150
  supervisor's evaluation, 151
  technological changes, 155
  vendor contacts, 152
Federal Library Resources Institute, 68
Federal Reserve Research Library, 85-106
  adjacent buildings, 85
  administrative support, 98
  automation manager, 91
  book selection, 92
  budget process, 93-95
  cataloger's role, 91
  CD-ROM resources and equipment, 100
  collection development, 92-93
  Committee on Library Functions, 88,101
  cooperative efforts, 101
  employee recognition, 104
  evaluation process, 103
  first librarian appointed, 88
  Friends of the Library, 93
  Government Depository Library, 88,92
  in-house computer network linkup, 89
  Innovative Interfaces Online Public Access Catalog (INNOPAC), 92,94

Federal Reserve Research Library
  (continued)
  interlibrary cooperation, 101
  librarian's responsibilities, 89
  library facilities, 98-100
  library technicians, 91
  management problems, 98
  management training, 96
  marketing techniques, 102-103
  National Library Week
    observance, 102
  National Monetary Commission
    book collection, 87
  networking, 100-101
  OCLC services, 88,91,100
  online databases, 100
  Operations Review teams, 103
  organizational chart, 90
  organizational structure, 89
  orientation sessions, 102
  Performance Management
    Program, 97
  periodical section, 91
  periodical subscription policy, 93
  personnel performance review,
    97-98
  photograph of, 86
  planning sessions, 95
  pleasant surroundings, 99-100
  program objectives, 94
  program planning, 95
  public service equipment, 99
  public use restriction, 93
  publicity, 102-103
  reader services, 89,91,99-100
  reading rooms, 99
  reference librarian's role, 91
  regional cooperation, 101
  retrospective cataloging, 89
  review process, 103
  special collections, 88
  staff involvement in planning, 95
  staff meetings, 96
  staff training, 96-97
  statistical information, 105-106

Federal Reserve Research Library
  (continued)
  student aide, 92
  subject coverage, 88
  teamwork, importance of, 104
  technical processing office, 91
  training courses, 96
  turnkey system for automation, 88
Federal Reserve System
  Board of Governors, 85,87
  establishment of, 85
  The Fed in Print, 101-102
  headquarters buildings, 85
  independent federal agency, 87
  Law Library, 87
  organizational structure, 87
  responsibilities, 87
  staff size, 87
  System Research Advisory
    Committee, 101
  union list of serials, 101
FEDLINK Network. *See* Federal
    Library and Information
    Center Committee
Funding, 27,67

Government Depository Library, 18,
    65,88,92

History of library, 10,61,129

Information dissemination, formal
    and informal, 71
Information services, 16,22
INNOPAC (Innovative Interfaces
    Online Public Access
    Catalog), 92,94
Integrated library systems, 26,67
Interlibrary loans, 72

Judicial Conference of the United
States
  governing body of federal
    judiciary, 36
  membership, 36
  national policies, 40-41
  personnel policies, 40-41,47
  policy setting, 36

LEGIS database, 9,22
Legislation tracking, 22
Library management, definition, 1
Library of Congress, optical disk
    system, 19. *See also*
    Congressional Research
    Service, National Library
    Service for the Blind
    and Physically Handicapped
Lister Hill National Center for
    Biomedical Communications,
    141-142

Management, 96,98,114-116,137
Marketing, 29,79,102
Military librarians
  percentage of federal librarians'
    workforce, 59
  professional activities, 58-59
  workshop, 58
Military libraries
  cooperative efforts, 58
  mission support, 57
  policy direction, 58

National Center for Biomedical
    Communications, Lister Hill,
    141-142
National Center for Biotechnology
    Information, 138-139,
    141,143

National Institutes of Health
  Human Genome program,
    138-139
  organization chart, 134-135
National libraries, 5
**National Library of Medicine,
129-146**
  access to online network, 136
  beginning of, 129
  bibliographic databases, 136
  Billings, John Shaw, 129
  Board of Regents, 137,139-140
  budget, 138
  CD-ROM products, 137
  collection size, 129
  communications research, 141
  DeBakey, Michael E., 140
  electronic imaging, 139
  Grateful Med program, 137,
    139-143
  Health Information Programs
    Development, Office of, 140
  high performance computing
    and communications, 141,
    143
  Index Medicus, 129,136
  information access, 140-142
  integrated access, 143
  international access, 137
  Lindberg, Donald A.B., 137,141
  Lister Hill National Center for
    Biomedical Communications,
    141-142
  Loansome Doc program, 137
  long range plan, 137-138,141
  management planning, 137
  medical library training, 139
  MEDLARS database, 136
  MEDLINE, 136,139
  naming of, 129
  National Network of Libraries
    of Medicine, 129,140
  National Research and Education
    Network (NREN), 141-142

National Library of Medicine
  (continued)
  network members by category,
    131
  network support, 131
  organization chart, 133
    See also National Institutes
      of Health, organization chart,
      134-135
  outreach planning panel, 140
  outreach program, 140
  Pepper, Claude, 139
  photos, 130,132
  regional medical libraries, 131
  research and development efforts,
    141
  statistical information, 145-146
  statistics, selected, 131
  TOXNET, 136
  Unified Medical Language
    System (UMLS), 142
  "Visible Human", 139,142
**National Library Service for
  the Blind and Physically
  Handicapped, 109-128**
  administrative responsibilities,
    114
  Administrative Section, 117
  audience for service, 109,121
  automation office, 117
  bibliographic control section, 119
  blind services authorized, 109
  blindness information, 111
  book selection, 110
  Braille Book Review, 110
  braille development section,
    119-120
  budget, formulation, 113
    preparation, 116
    staff involvement, 116
  Collection Development Section,
    120
  congressional appropriations, 110
  consumer relations officer,
    111,121

National Library Service for
  the Blind and Physically
  Handicapped *(continued)*
  contact list, 118
  contracting responsibility
    of director, 114
  copyright permissions, 109
  director's responsibilities, 113-114
  eligibility requirements for
    services, 110
  Engineering Section, 120
  Inventory Management Section,
    124
  legal authorization, 109
  liaison with individuals
    and organizations, 112
  library service network (chart),
    122
  major service centers (chart), 123
  Management Plan, 116
    Review and Analysis Program,
      participation in, 114
    study, 114,115
  materials, custodian of all relevant
    reading, 112
    Development Division, 119
    music, 111
    scope of, 109
  monitoring network of libraries,
    112,121
  Music Section, 124
  national network of regional
    libraries, 109,121
  Network Division, 121
    Services Section, 124
  organizational structure, 118
  participatory management, 115
  performance goals for
    administrators, 115
  periodicals available, 110
  physically impaired included
    by law, 109
  playback equipment availability,
    110
  postage-free mail, 109

National Library Service for the Blind and Physically Handicapped *(continued)*
   production control section, 120
   program, planning
      and development, 113
      responsibilities, 112
   Publications and Media Section, 117
   Quality Assurance Section, 121
   Recording Studio, 120-121
   Reference Section, 124-125
   representative to related national and international organizations, 113
   Research and Development Officer, 117,119
      programs, 111
   service philosophy, 125
   Spanish language books, 110
   staff meetings, 115-116
   statistics, general information, 127-128
      growth, 116-117
   Talking Book Topics, 110
   Taylor Street Annex headquarters, 114
   union catalog availability, 110
   volunteer training, 111
Networking, 100-101,121,124,131

One person libraries, 5
Online Computer Library Center (OCLC), 25,39,88,91,100
Online services, 92,94,100
Organization charts. *See* entries under individual libraries
Outreach, 29,139-141

Patient libraries, 5
Pentagon Library, 61-70
   access policy, 63-64
   action officers as customers, 62-63

Pentagon Library *(continued)*
   Army Library Institute, 59-60,68
   Army support, 61
   automated acquisition subsystem, 65
   CD-ROM local area network, 67
   Circulation Service, 65
   collection, scope of, 64
   consolidation of many libraries, 61
   Defense Library on Disc, 67
   departmental library, 57
   Federal Library and Information Center Committee (FLICC) representative, 62
   Federal Library Resources Institute, 68
   FEDLINK network, 68
   funding, 67
   government depository library, 65
   historical development, 61
   Integrated Library System, 67
   interns, training of, 68
   manager's responsibilities, 61-62
   Marshall, George C., 61
   Metcalf Study, 61
   MILDOCS On Disc, 67
   Military References and Resources, 68
   naming of, 61
   no-growth policy, 65
   organizational structure and chart, 66
   patrons, 62-63
   Pentagon Library Users System (PLUS), 65,67
   photos of, 62-64
   procurement problems, 68
   Research and Information Services division, 65
   staff, size, 65
      training, 68
   statistical information, 69-70
   Technical Services Division, 65
   tours, 68

Periodicals, 19,91,93,110
Photos. *See* entries under individual libraries
Planning, 27,72,75,95
Presidential Libraries, 4
Prison Libraries, 5
Publicity, 102-103

Redstone Scientific Information Center, 71-82
accessibility, 72
administrative supervision, 76
Army High School Faculty Math/Science Program, 79
Army's research, development and engineering center facility, 76
largest scientific and technical information facility, 71
budget process, 75-76
central research library, 72
computerized functions, 77
cooperative education program, 78
director's responsibilities, 76
establishment in 1960s, 71
evaluation techniques, 80
five-year plan, 75
governing board, 75
historical background, 71-72
Huntsville, Alabama headquarters, 71
interlibrary loans, 72
intern program, 78
marketing techniques, 79
mission, 72
multi-agency facility, 76
1961 study, 72
one-stop information service, 77
organizational structure, 76
patrons, 71-72,77
photos, 73-74
planning, 72,75
research and development collection, 71

Redstone Scientific Information Center *(continued)*
scientific and technical information dissemination, 71
special services, 77
staff training, 77-78
statistical information, 81-82
STILAS system, 77
technician training, 78
teleconferences, 78
translation services, 71,78
user services, 77
Reference service, 9,21-22
Research and development programs, 117,119,141
Retrospective cataloging, 23,89

Satellite libraries, 38,43-45,48
School libraries, 5
Scientific and technical libraries, 5
Sixth Circuit Judicial Conference, library review, 46
Sixth Circuit Library System, 35-54
autonomy, relative, 48
branch libraries, 43-45,48
centralized book ordering, 44
Cincinnati, Ohio headquarters, 35,43
coordination of services, 45
courts served, 46
discretionary authority, 48
expansion in 1980s, 44
Federal court direction, 49-50
four-state coverage, 43-44
historical background, 43-44
judicial autonomy, 35
library advisory committees, 46
Library Judges, 46
library staff, 44
main facility, 44
matrix-type supervision, 47
mission, 45
organizational structure, 47
chart, 51-52

Sixth Circuit Library System
(*continued*)
  regional control, 44
  statistical information, 53-54
  See also Federal Circuit Library System
Special Libraries Association, Military Librarians Division, 58
Staff. *See* entries under individual libraries
Statistical Information. *See* entries under individual libraries
STILAS (Scientific and Technical Information Library Automation System), 77
Systems specialist, 1-2

Technical services, 16,23,65,91

U.S. Army libraries, 57-60
  cohesiveness and cooperation, 59
  Electronic Gateway (EGAL), 60
  military history institute, 57
  1976 adjutant general study, 59
  See also Army headings, Pentagon Library, Redstone Scientific Information Center, military headings
U.S. Capitol, photo, 11
U.S. Court of Appeals for the Sixth Circuit, 35-54
  circuit court policy, 46
  library committee, 46
  organization, 45
  Potter Stewart Building, 35
    photo of, 37
U.S. Courts
  Article III judges, 46-47
  budgeting, decentralized, 42
  facilities management, 41

U.S. Courts (*continued*)
  General Services Administration, 41
  Guide to Judiciary Policies and Procedures, 36
  jurisdiction, 35
  librarian appointments, 47
  national library program, 35-36, 38-39
  See also Administrative Office of the U.S. Courts, Federal Circuit Library System, Sixth Circuit Library System
U.S. Department of Defense, library support, 57
  See also Pentagon Library, Redstone Scientific Information Center
U.S. House of Representatives
  House Information Services (HIS) databases, 25
  printed documents collection, 18
U.S. Judicial Conference, 36,40-41
U.S. Senate
  comprehensive budget, 28
  computer center, 24
  disbursing office, 29
  organizational chart, 14-15
  printed documents collection, 18
U.S. Senate Library, 9-32
  annual report, 27
  automation history, 24
  book collection, 9,19
  budgeting cycle, 27
  CD-ROM capabilities, 19,26
  circulation service, 23
  collection development, policy and preservation, 10,17-20
  commercial databases available, 25
  computerized catalog, 23
  Congressional Research Service (CRS), 21
  products file, 26

U.S. Senate Library, Congressional
  Research Service *(continued)*
  public policy literature
    database, 26
  disaster preparedness
    and recovery plan, 20
  document collection, 10
  early expansion, 10
  Federal Library and Information
    Center Committee (FLICC)
    member, 25
  fiber optical network link, 26
  functional areas, 9,16
  funding: budget
    and appropriations, 27-28
  government depository library, 18
  government publications, 19
  Hickey, William, 10
  history, 10
  Hot Bills List, 30
  hours of operation, 21
  informal tours, 29
  information services, 16,22
  in-house automated circulation
    system, 26
  integrated library system
    (Datatrek), 26
  journalists, 21
  legal materials, 10,18
  LEGIS: service, staff, usage, 9,22
  Legislative branch appropriations,
    27
  legislative records, 17-18
  Library of Congress, relationship
    with, 21,26
  marketing, 29
  microform collection, 19,24
  micrographics center, 19,23-24
  mission, 9
  new technologies, 10
  non-partisan services, 22
  non-print materials, 19
  off-site storage, 12,20

U.S. Sentate Library *(continued)*
  Online Computer Library Center
    (OCLC), 25
  optical disk technology, 26
  organizational chart, 13
  original location, 12
  outreach programs, 29
  patronage, pre-1970, 16
  patrons, 20
  performance evaluation, 16
  periodicals collections, 19
  personnel evaluation, 17
  photo of (U.S. Capitol), 11
  planning, 27
  Presidential Vetoes, 1789-1991,
    30
  printed documents collection, 18
  promotional mailings, 30
  publications program, 30
  reference collection policy, 18
  reference service, 9,21-22
  relocation plans, 12
  requests, types of, 22
  Resources Directory, 30
  retrospective cataloging, 23
  SCORPIO database, 25
  Secretary of the Senate,
    jurisdiction, 12
  Senators' Reading Room, 12,23
  space allocation, 12
  staff: recruitment, selection,
    training, 16-17
  statistical information, 31-32
  supervision, 16
  technical services and support,
    16,23
  U.S. Congressional Serial Set, 18
  users, groups and services, 20-21
  seminars, 29
  video collection, 19
  voucher system, 29
  Wagner, George S., 10
User services, 21,65,67,77